The
Lucent
Library
of
Historical
Eras

Arts, Leisure, and Entertainment: Life of the Ancient Romans

Other titles in the Lucent Library of Historical Eras, Ancient Rome, include:

From Founding to Fall: A History of Rome
Influential Figures of Ancient Rome
The Roman Army: A Instrument of Power
Words of the Ancient Romans: Primary Sources

The Lucent Library of Historical Eras

Arts, Leisure, and Entertainment: Life of the Ancient Romans

Don Nardo

LUCENT
BOOKS®

THOMSON
GALE

San Diego • Detroit • New York • San Francisco • Cleveland • New Haven, Conn. • Waterville, Maine • London • Munich

LIBRARY OF CONGRESS CATALOGING-IN-PUBLICATION DATA

Nardo, Don, 1947–
   Arts, leisure, and entertainment: life of the ancient Romans / By Don Nardo.
     p. cm.—(The Lucent library of historical eras. Ancient Rome)
   SUMMARY: An overview of Rome's Leisure Pursuits, dinners, the theater, literature,
games and sports, and chariot races and battles.
Includes bibliographical references and index.
  ISBN 1-59018-317-7 (hardback : alk. paper)
  1. Rome—Social life and customs. 2. Leisure—Rome. I. Title. II. Series.
DG78.N37 2004
306.4'8'0937—dc21

2003007625

Printed in the United States of America

Contents

Foreword

Looking back from the vantage point of the present, history can be viewed as a myriad of intertwining roads paved by human events. Some paths stand out—broad highways whose mileposts, even from a distance of centuries, are clear. The events that propelled the rise to power of Germany's Third Reich, its role in World War II, and its eventual demise, for example, are well defined and documented.

Other roads are less distinct, their route sometimes hidden from view. Modern legislatures may have developed from old tribal councils, for example, but the links between them are indistinct in places, open to discussion and interpretation.

The architecture of civilization—law, religion, art, science, and government—as well as the more everyday aspects of our culture—what we eat, what we wear—all developed along the historical roads and byways. In that progression can be traced every facet of modern life.

A broad look back along these roads reveals that many paths—though of vastly different character—seem to converge at a few critical junctions. These intersections are those great historical eras that echo over the long, steady course of human history, extending beyond the past and into the present.

These epic periods of time are the focus of Lucent's Library of Historical Eras. They shine through the mists of history like beacons, illuminated by a burst of creativity that propels events forward—so bright that we, from thousands of years away, can clearly see the chain of events leading to the present.

Each Lucent Library of Historical Eras consists of a set of books that highlight various aspects of these major eras. For example, the Elizabethan England library features volumes on Queen Elizabeth I and her court, Elizabethan theater, the great playwrights, and everyday life in Elizabethan London.

The minilibrary approach allows for the division of each era into its most significant and most interesting parts and the exploration of those parts in depth. Also, social and cultural trends as well as illustrative documents and eyewitness accounts can be prominently featured in individual volumes.

Lucent's Library of Historical Eras presents a wealth of information to young readers. The lively narrative, fully documented primary and secondary source quotations, maps, photographs, sidebars, and annotated bibliographies serve as launching points for class discussion and further research.

In studying the great historical eras, students also develop a better understanding of our own times. What we learn from the past and how we apply it in the present may shape the future and may determine whether our era will be a guiding light to those traveling future roads.

Introduction:
How Do We Know About Roman Leisure Pursuits?

Entertainment and leisure pastimes underwent a profound revolution during the twentieth century. Almost all cities and towns in the world's industrialized nations now have movie theaters. And nearly all homes have televisions, radios, stereos, computers, VCRs, and DVD players. Cars, trains, and airplanes, which allow people to travel fast and vacation far away, are also everywhere and taken for granted. These ingenious and compelling devices are often the focus of leisure time activities enjoyed by people of all walks of life.

The ancients, of course, including the Romans, lacked these modern marvels. So if a person could travel back in time from present-day Rome to ancient Rome, he or she might feel somewhat disconcerted by the lack of automation, the reliance on muscle and animal power for most tasks, and the slower pace of life. The time traveler would also probably be disturbed, perhaps even repulsed, by the carnage of the Roman arena. There, gladiators and animals fought to the death while crowds of spectators cheered and often, with the turn of a thumb, helped decide who would live or die.

On the other hand, the time traveler would find some of the leisure pursuits the Romans engaged in quite familiar and entertaining. They went out to dinner, for example, and threw dinner parties, both small and large, at home. Romans also attended live plays in theaters, live recitations and musical performances, museums and art exhibits, horse races, and boxing and wrestling matches. They hunted, fished, gambled, and played ball and board games. And those who were literate wrote or read poetry, histories, letters, novels, and other types of popular literature.

The Literary Evidence

Our imaginary time traveler would know exactly what the Romans did to amuse themselves and how they did it because he or she would see it firsthand. Unfortunately, historians and other interested people today do not enjoy that advantage. Some fifteen centuries have elapsed since Rome's fall. During that long interval, the remnants of Roman civilization have substantially decayed. Therefore, much about Roman life has been lost or forgotten. How, then, do historians and other scholars know about everyday Roman life, including popular entertainments and leisure pastimes?

Fortunately, the quest to reconstruct and understand how the Romans lived has been facilitated by two major kinds of evidence. First is the literary evidence. Although large portions of the writings of the ancient Greeks and Romans are forever lost, some have survived. Of these, a certain proportion, particularly histories, biographies, letters, and legal documents, are fairly straightforward and reliable in their descriptions of events, personalities, ideas, and customs. For example, the first-century A.D. historian Tacitus describes how thousands of people were killed in the collapse of a wooden amphitheater.

Members of a wealthy Roman family enjoy some leisure time in the spacious courtyard of their townhouse. Archaeologists have excavated the remains of such homes.

From this account, we learn that gladiatorial fights and wild beast shows sometimes took place in makeshift wooden structures that could be dangerous to the spectators. Similarly, an older contemporary of Tacitus, the playwright Seneca, lived above a public bath. In one of his surviving letters, he complains about being kept awake by incessant noise, including grunting weightlifters and people splashing in the swimming pool. This shows that such facilities featured exercise rooms and swimming pools.

Some other kinds of writings, particularly satires, though sometimes helpful, are less reliable. In the words of J.P.V.D. Balsdon, a noted expert on Roman leisure life, the works of satirists like Juvenal and Martial (both of the first century A.D.) must "be handled with extreme care." These writers, he points out,

> were interested in a very particular and very limited world, in the things in which society people gossiped about and . . . ill-bred and ill-behaved people committed. They avoided . . . writing about things and people that were tediously dull—about ordinary people, in fact. A satirist, like a cartoonist, must distort. Therefore, within their limited field they are not to be treated as simple purveyors of truth.[1]

Still, Martial and Juvenal open fascinating windows on ancient Roman society if one is careful to filter out the frequent exaggerations, moralizing, and so forth. Martial, for instance, drops numerous tantalizing

This drawing of the historian Tacitus is based on a surviving bust.

and useful bits of information about Roman food, dining habits, and public games while criticizing or romanticizing them.

The Archaeological Evidence

The other major type of evidence for Roman leisure life comes from archaeological excavations or preservations. The most obvious example consists of the ruins of theaters, racetracks, gymnasiums, bathhouses, villas, and other structures. Part of the Circus Maximus, Rome's largest racetrack, has been excavated, for instance, and the foundations and some of the columns and walls of the great Baths of Caracalla, also in Rome, can still be seen by tourists. These tangible remains show the impressive size and dimensions of these once immense structures. (The Circus Maximus sat at least 150,000 people, and Caracalla's baths accommodated up to 10,000 bathers at a time.) Excavations of smaller, more modest buildings, such as villas and townhouses, reveal dining rooms, private baths, ball courts, and roof-covered patios where the owners lounged or entertained guests. Archaeology has also yielded examples of the furnishings of these structures, as well as personal items—toiletries, jewelry, dinnerware, and the like—belonging to those who lived in them.

Other kinds of valuable artifacts revealed by archaeology include art objects such as sculptures, wall and vase paintings, and mosaics. Surviving statues depict wrestlers, jockeys, and other athletes. Stone bas-reliefs show hunters, charioteers, boxers, and gladiators engaged in their peculiar pursuits as well as dinner parties and tavern scenes. Paintings and mosaics illustrate actors on the stage, gladiators, circus events, and much more. Especially striking are the examples found at Pompeii and Herculaneum, two small Roman cities buried and largely preserved by the ash laid down by the volcano Mount Vesuvius in its famous eruption of August A.D. 79.

Another kind of archaeological evidence found at Pompeii is graffiti, informal words and drawings painted or scratched onto walls. One of these announces, "The gladiatorial troop hired by Aulus Suettius Certus will fight in Pompeii on May 31. There will also be a wild animal hunt. The awnings

In this Roman mosaic, the gladiator on the left, named Astinax, has become entangled in the net of his opponent, Knendio. In an accompanying panel, Knendio is defeated.

will be used."[2] This single, short blurb conveys much information about Roman public games: that individuals, as well as the state, paid for games; that gladiators and animal acts appeared on the same program; that awnings shielded the spectators from the bright sun; and, of course, that a major way of advertising the games was by hand-painted ads like this one.

Graffiti was only one of many types of inscription. An inscription consists of words carved or scratched into a durable material such as stone, metal, wood, tile, earthenware, or glass. About three hundred thousand Roman inscriptions (excluding those on coins) have been discovered, and new ones are found each year. Among the more widely noted recent examples is an invitation to a birthday party etched into a wooden writing tablet. It was found in the ruins of a Roman fort at Vindolanda, near Hadrian's Wall, in Britain (which was once a Roman province). "Greetings," the wife of the commander of a neighboring fort tells Sulpicia Lepidina, wife of Vindolanda's commander.

> For the day of the celebration of my birthday, I give you a warm invitation to make sure you come to us, to make the day more enjoyable for me by your arrival, if you come. Give my greetings to your [husband] Cerialis. My [husband] Aelius and my little son send you their greeting.[3]

Other kinds of inscriptions relating to Roman leisure life include lists of victories earned by chariot drivers, tablets containing curses directed from one athlete to a rival, and tomb epitaphs providing the names of singers, dancers, musicians, music teachers, actresses, horse racers, and many others.

Piecing together and correlating the literary and archaeological evidence creates an admittedly imperfect yet fairly detailed and reliable picture of Roman entertainments and leisure pursuits. It is an illuminating, sometimes disturbing, but always fascinating picture, to be sure. The Romans were, on the whole, an austere, conservative people who could be very preoccupied with and serious about war, legal matters, achieving social status, and making a living. But the evidence shows clearly that they also liked to relax and have fun. That makes it easier for people today to identify with them, despite the great gulfs of time and culture that separate then from now.

The Roman Baths

It would be difficult to single out a single leisure pastime that most preoccupied the Romans throughout their history. This is partly because that history was extremely long and eventful and saw continual changes in Rome's political and military situation as well as in the social attitudes, customs, and habits of its people. From its legendary founding in 753 B.C. to its fall in A.D. 476, for example, Rome experienced various kinds of rulers. These included a line of kings (the Monarchy, 753–509 B.C.), a Senate and elected officials (the Republic, 509–30 B.C.), and a series of autocratic emperors (the Empire, 30 B.C.–A.D. 476). And from the Monarchy to the early Empire, Rome itself evolved from a small, unimpressive city with unpaved streets and wooden buildings to a sprawling metropolis of stone, polished marble, and a million inhabitants—the capital of the known world.

Meanwhile, as the initially tiny Roman city-state grew, conquered all of Italy, and then acquired a huge overseas empire, many and diverse peoples came under Roman rule. The religions, customs, pastimes, and entertainments of these peoples, most especially the Greeks, left their imprint on Roman culture. Various customs and pastimes that had not been fashionable in Rome during the Monarchy and early Republic became acceptable and widely practiced later as a result of foreign cultural influences.

The most notable example in this regard was communal bathing, both private

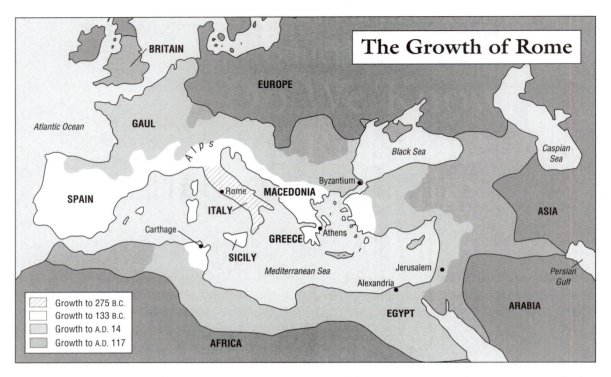

The Growth of Rome

BRITAIN

EUROPE

Atlantic Ocean

GAUL

Alps

SPAIN

ITALY

•Rome   MACEDONIA

Carthage

SICILY

GREECE   Athens

Mediterranean Sea

Byzantium

Black Sea

Caspian Sea

ASIA

Jerusalem •

Alexandria

Persian Gulf

ARABIA

EGYPT

AFRICA

Growth to 275 B.C.
Growth to 133 B.C.
Growth to A.D. 14
Growth to A.D. 117

and public. From the first century B.C. on, visiting the baths on an almost daily basis was probably the most common Roman leisure pastime, one that people of nearly all walks of life enjoyed. This situation stood in marked contrast with that of prior centuries. The early Romans had bathed rather infrequently, and their bathing facilities, if they can be called such, had been crude. Those inclined to wash usually did so in a river or stream or poured buckets of water into a small tub made of wood or terra-cotta (baked clay). Another method was to rub oil (usually olive oil) onto the skin and scrape it off, along with dirt and sweat, with a strigil, a curved utensil made of wood, bone, or metal.

After coming into close contact with the Greeks during the second century B.C., however, the Romans began to adopt the custom of communal bathing. Many Romans resisted this at first. A common view was that Greek luxuries and social customs, including public bathing and competing in athletics, were soft, unmanly, and frivolous and would surely corrupt the moral fiber of Roman society. The historian Tacitus later summed up this attitude, writing:

Traditional morals, already gradually deteriorating, have been utterly ruined by this imported laxity [moral looseness]! It makes everything potentially corrupting and corruptible flow into the capital, [as] foreign influences demoralize our young men into shirkers, gymnasts, and [sexual] perverts. . . . Good behavior has no time left for it. In these promiscuous crowds, debauchees [immoral people] are emboldened to practice by night the lusts they have imagined by day.[4]

This fourth-century B.C. Etruscan oil flask and strigil belonged to an athlete.

Because of this deeply ingrained conservative attitude, some Greek leisure pursuits never caught on in Rome. But communal bathing was one that did, despite the initial naysayers. In fact, the Romans, who were known for their habit of borrowing and building on ideas from other cultures, carried the notion of bathhouses to new heights. Eventually, thousands of them were erected in Rome and other cities across the realm; and many of these structures were far larger and more luxurious than anything ever dreamed of in the Greek world.

The Early Bathhouses

At first, Rome's communal bathhouses were referred to as *balneae* (the plural of *balneum*). As a rule, these were small, spare, privately run, and open only to members. The larger public baths later built and maintained by the state became known as *thermae* (the plural of *thermarum*), although the two terms may eventually have become more or less interchangeable.

The owner of a small private bathhouse commonly hired a *balneator*, or "bathman," to run the establishment. Sometimes the owner leased the building to a middle man, who then hired the *balneator*. A surviving graffito at Pompeii advertises the latter situation, in which a well-to-do woman offers to lease her property:

On the estate of Julia Felix, the daughter of Spurius Felix, the following are for rent: an elegant bath suitable for the best people, shops, rooms above them, and second story apartments, from the Ides of August [August 15] until the

Ides of August five years hence, after which the lease may be renewed by simple agreement.[5]

In cases in which the owner was very wealthy and of a charitable nature, admittance to a *balneum* might be free. Otherwise, there was a modest charge.

The earliest bathhouses, which appeared in Rome during the second century B.C., were not only small but also featured modest facilities by later standards. They likely consisted of a few rooms, each with a few old-fashioned bathtubs and perhaps one or two slightly larger sunken pools. These receptacles were of necessity small because they had to be filled and emptied by hand, a job that kept a small staff of slaves constantly busy. Also, for a hot bath, water had to be warmed in kettles over a fire; it must have taken quite a bit of time and effort to fill even a small bathing pool with hot water and keep it hot.

A Bathhouse in a Mining Colony

The surviving inscription excerpted here, dating from the second century, comes from a Roman mining colony in Lusitania (now Portugal). As quoted in volume 2 of Lewis and Reinhold's Roman Civilization, *the fragment consists of part of the agreement between the government official running the colony and a businessman who had purchased a lease to run the local bathhouse. (The facility was for the use of the Romans who ran the mine, along with their staffs, families, and personal slaves, not the slaves and convicts who did the actual work.)*

The lessee of the baths . . . shall, in accordance with the terms of his lease running to June 30 next, be required to heat the baths and keep them open for use entirely at his own expense everyday from daybreak to the seventh hour for women, and from the eighth hour to the second hour in the evening for men. . . . He shall be required to provide a proper supply of running water for the heated rooms, to the bath tub up to the highest level and to the basin. . . . The lessee shall charge men one half *as* each and women one *as* each. Imperial freedmen or slaves in the service of the procurator . . . are admitted free; likewise minors and soldiers. At the expiration of the lease, the lessee . . . shall be required to return in good condition all the bath equipment consigned to him, excepting any rendered unusable through age. . . . If the baths are not properly kept open for use, then the procurator of the mines shall have the right to fine the lessee up to 200 *sesterces* every time they are not kept open properly.

This nineteenth-century Italian engraving reconstructs a tepidarium *(warm room for working up a sweat) in a public bath at Pompeii.*

This situation changed markedly following the invention of the hypocaust, an ingenious heating system that may have been invented by a Roman businessman, Gaius Sergius Orata, around 100 B.C. In the most common version of the system, a house, bathhouse, palace, or other structure was erected over a shallow cellar and was supported by brick or concrete piers (vertical supports) two to three feet high. Brick channels connected the cellar to a furnace located several feet away from the building. Slaves tended the furnace, making sure that it was well supplied with wood or some other fuel. As warm air from the furnace circulated through the channels, it gradually heated the building's ground floor, which was made of concrete, a material that efficiently retains heat. In some more elaborate versions of the hypocaust, which were installed in larger bathhouses, warm air also circulated into hollow spaces in some of the walls.

Thanks to the boon of heat supplied by hypocausts, large-scale bathhouses equipped with complex facilities rapidly spread across the Roman world. As time went on, increasing numbers of these, particularly the largest ones, were public versions financed by the government. By the middle of the reign of the first emperor, Augustus (30 B.C.–A.D. 14), the city of Rome alone had more than 170 bathhouses; by the time of

The underground channels of a hypocaust are visible beneath a mosaic tile floor in the remains of a wealthy Roman villa in Britain.

the playwright Seneca and noted diplomat and letter writer Pliny the Younger (mid-to-late first century A.D.), there were perhaps double that number. And by the Empire's last century, Rome boasted more than 900 bathhouses.

These establishments ranged widely in size, attractiveness, and quality of service. Some were seedy little places that were little more than fronts for brothels, but many others were cleaner and more respectable. A few were huge, palacelike structures adorned with magnificent art treasures. Among the latter were the baths of Agrippa, Nero, Titus, Trajan, Caracalla, Diocletian, and Constantine. Caracalla's baths, erected in the early third century A.D., took some nine thousand workmen more than five years to erect. The complex measured 1,107 by 1,104 feet, and its interior ceilings were supported by 252 columns, 16 of which were about 5 feet in diameter, more than 40 feet high, and weighed 50 tons each.

The Frequency and Cost of Attendance

Bathhouses became such an important institution in Rome because a large proportion of the population attended them instead of bathing at home. Not surprisingly, the major exception was well-to-do persons who could afford to install and maintain elaborate bathing facilities in their houses. For various reasons, many of these individuals did visit the communal baths on a pe-

riodic basis; but when they desired peace and quiet, or to bathe after dark (when the communal baths were closed), their home baths were a welcome retreat.

For example, Pliny the Younger had a luxurious country villa near Ostia, Rome's port (about fifteen miles west of the capital). In a letter to a friend, he describes his private bathing suite, which included several small specialized chambers and a swimming pool, all heated by a hypocaust, which Pliny refers to as the "furnace-room."

[Behind a series of bedrooms, one finds] the cooling-room of the bath, which is large and spacious and has two

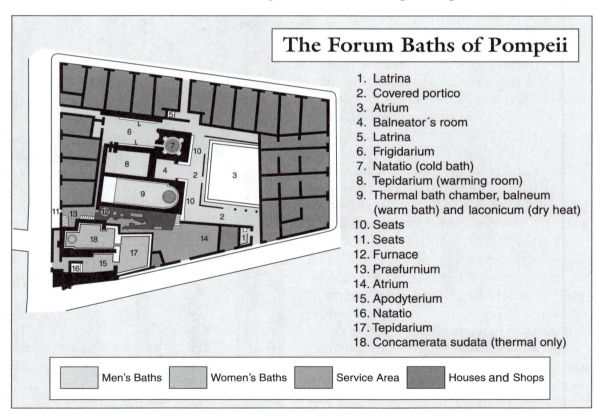

The Forum Baths of Pompeii

1. Latrina
2. Covered portico
3. Atrium
4. Balneator´s room
5. Latrina
6. Frigidarium
7. Natatio (cold bath)
8. Tepidarium (warming room)
9. Thermal bath chamber, balneum (warm bath) and laconicum (dry heat)
10. Seats
11. Seats
12. Furnace
13. Praefurnium
14. Atrium
15. Apodyterium
16. Natatio
17. Tepidarium
18. Concamerata sudata (thermal only)

Men's Baths   Women's Baths   Service Area   Houses and Shops curved baths [large tubs] built out of opposite walls; these are quite large enough if you consider that the sea is so near. Next come the oiling-room [where bathers oiled and strigiled], the furnace-room, and the antechamber to the bath, and then two rest-rooms [toilet stalls], beautifully decorated in a simple style, leading to the heated swimming-bath, which is much admired and from which swimmers can see the sea.[6]

Pliny goes on to say that when he lacked the time or inclination to heat up his private baths, he patronized one of three small public baths in a nearby village.

Most Romans were not as well off as Pliny, of course, so they consistently relied on the public baths. As for how often they attended, it depended a great deal on personal preference. Some people went every day or even several times a day. One ancient source claims that the emperor Gordian I (reigned 238) bathed five times a day in the summer and twice a day in the winter. (It is likely that a fair number of these baths took place in his private facilities.) At the other extreme was Augustus, the first emperor, who bathed rarely, especially in the winter. He preferred to apply oil and strigil or to sweat in front of a fire and then have a slave pour a bucket of lukewarm water over him.

These high-ranking individuals aside, it is difficult to tell how often people of average or less-than-average means attended the baths since most of the surviving information about Roman social customs describes members of the upper classes. But the sheer number and size of the bathhouses in Rome and other cities imply a large number of regular customers. Two to five visits a week for the average person seems plausible. The cost was certainly low enough for

A reconstruction of the magnificent entrance hall of the Baths of Caracalla, built in the third century A.D.

Lucian's Guide to a Roman Bath

This excerpt from the Greek writer Lucian's description of a large Roman bath (quoted in Jo-Ann Shelton's As the Romans Did *) takes the reader on a partial tour, beginning in the locker rooms.*

Beyond [the lobby and meeting rooms] are two spacious locker rooms and, between them, a lofty and brightly lit hall which contains three cold-water swimming pools. It is decorated with slabs of Laconian marble and with two white marble statues. . . . Upon leaving this hall, you enter into a large room which is long, rounded at each end, and slightly warm, rather than being confronted suddenly with intense heat. Beyond this room and to the right is a very bright room which is quite suitably arranged for rub-downs with oil. At each end it has an entranceway decorated with Phrygian marble to provide access for those coming in from the exercise area. And then near this room is another large room, the most beautiful of all rooms, very well designed for standing about or sitting down, for whiling away time without fear of reproach, or for occupying your time most profitably. It, too, gleams from top to bottom with Phrygian marble.

even the poorest Romans to attend often; the entrance fee for adults at the large public baths was only a *quadrans* (a quarter of an *as*, a common unit of Roman currency), equivalent to pocket change today. Considering what the patron received in return, this was an exceptionally reasonable deal. What is more, children were admitted free. The oil used for strigiling was more expensive, but sometimes wealthy private benefactors subsidized this cost. In the early third century, the government began supplying the oil for free to bathers.

These bathers were both male and female, so mixed bathing was always an issue that bathhouse owners and the gov-

ernment had to address. Apparently only the cheapest and least respectable establishments allowed men and women to bathe together. Most bathhouses offered separate facilities for women, which were adjacent to the men's so that both could be heated by the same hypocaust. Or they staggered their hours so that men and women attended at different times; usually the women went in the morning, the men in the afternoon.

From Warm to Hot to Cold

When entering one of the larger *thermae*, these patrons slowly made their way through a series of connected rooms. First came one or more lobbies or reception and meeting

A nineteenth-century watercolor captures the splendor of one of the chambers within a large Roman bathhouse. Note the openings to admit light.

rooms, usually quite spacious, as described by the second-century Greek writer Lucian after visiting a large Roman bathhouse:

> The entrance is high, with a flight of broad steps of which the tread [horizontal surface] is greater than the pitch [vertical surface], to make them easy to ascend. On entering, one is received into a public hall of good size with ample accommodations for servants and attendants. On the left are the lounging rooms . . . attractive, brightly lighted retreats. Then, beside them, [is] a hall, larger than need be for the purposes of a bath, but necessary for the reception of richer persons.[7]

From the lobby or reception rooms, patrons entered a room for undressing and dressing, the *apodyterium*. It had benches as well as cubicles to store the bathers' clothes and other personal items. In the better establishments, these items were probably guarded by slaves.

On leaving the *apodyterium,* most patrons entered the *tepidarium,* a warm room without a bath, where they remained until they started perspiring. Then a bather commonly followed one of several possible routines. He or she might enter the *caldarium,* a hot room with one or more pools of hot water. In the large bathhouse Lucian visited, the corridor leading to the hot room was "faced with Numidian marble. The hall beyond it is very beautiful, full of abundant light and aglow with color. . . . It contains three hot tubs." [8] The patron might follow the session in the hot room with a visit to the *frigidarium,* a room with one or more pools of cold water. He or she might then dry off with woolen towels brought from home. Well-to-do bathers brought slaves, who toweled off their masters.

Another alternative was for the patron to go from the *tepidarium* into a saunalike dry room, the *laconicum,* and there work up a profuse sweat. He or she might then go on to the *frigidarium* for a cold dip, followed by a toweling; or the person might

A drawing of a frigidarium *(room containing a pool of cold water). Archaeologists discovered the chamber almost intact in the remains of a bathhouse at Pompeii.*

enter the *unctorium,* or "oil room," where oiling, strigiling, and massages took place. Most bathers carried their oil in small flasks (*ampullae*). Those who could afford it had their own slaves oil and strigil them, and slaves provided by the establishment did the massages. A quaint story has survived describing some visits made by the emperor Hadrian (reigned 117–138) to the *unctorium* of a public bathhouse:

> On one occasion he [Hadrian] had seen a certain veteran, known to him in military service, rubbing his back and the rest of his body on the wall; he asked why he had the marble scrape him, and when he learned that this was done for the reason that he [the veteran] did not have a slave, he [Hadrian] presented him both with slaves and with the cost of their maintenance. But on another day when several old men were rubbing themselves on the wall to arouse the emperor's generosity, he ordered them to be called out and to rub each other down in turn. [9]

Bathers might follow still other routines during their visits to the bathhouses. Some went back and forth from the hot pools to the cold ones several times before getting oiled or massaged. And others skipped the *unctorium* altogether in favor of lounging or doing laps in a large swimming pool (*natatio*), which was often heated. Whatever routine a patron chose to follow, he or she

Boozers in the Baths

People not only ate meals and snacks in the bathhouses but also drank wine, unfortunately sometimes to excess, which must have irritated the sober patrons. In this epigram the humorist Martial (from D.R. Shackleton Bailey's translation) describes a fellow who severely criticized drinking too much in the baths when he was poor but then became an offender himself after inheriting a fortune.

Not long ago, when a bow-legged, home-bred slave carried Aper's towels and a one-eyed old woman sat watching over his little gown and a ruptured masseur handed him his drop of oil, he was a stern, harsh censor of boozers. He would shout that the cups should be smashed and the [wine] poured away which a knight, fresh from his bath, was imbibing [drinking]. But now that 300,000 [sesterces] has come his way from an aged uncle, he doesn't know how to go home from the baths sober. Oh, what a difference open-work [expensive] goblets and five long-haired boys [Aper's new slaves] can make! When Aper was poor, he wasn't thirsty!

must have been extremely clean and relaxed on leaving the facility.

Meeting Friends, Exercising, and Eating

As appealing as these facilities sound, the larger *thermae* were much more than places where Romans perspired, washed, and swam. They were also busy social centers. On the one hand, many people gathered in a bathhouse to meet friends, either in the reception halls, the bathing facilities, or elsewhere in the facility. Others mixed business with pleasure, either by meeting with business associates, clients, or patrons, or by bringing work with them. (Clients were socially and often financially dependent on patrons and were expected to do favors for them and meet them at specified times and places.) Meeting a patron could sometimes be a chore for a client, especially if the client had to go to a bathhouse he normally did not frequent in order to keep his patron happy. "I must always wait upon you shivering at the crack of dawn," the humorist Martial tells his patron in an epigram (short poem). "At the tenth hour or later I must wearily follow you to Agrippa's baths, though I myself use Titus's. Have I deserved this . . . to be forever a raw recruit to your friendship?"[10] Martial also describes a man who frequently followed him to the baths and incessantly recited verses, prompting Martial to flee the premises. And the noted scholar Pliny the Elder (the uncle of Pliny the Younger), a workaholic, brought along his secretary so that he could dictate information while being oiled and massaged.

People also went to the larger bathhouses to exercise and play games. In addition to its extensive bathing facilities, such a complex featured indoor and outdoor exercise rooms and gyms (*palaestrae*), where people played handball and *harpastum* (a rough-and-tumble ball game similar to rugby), wrestled, and lifted weights. Ballplayers, weight lifters, and divers highlight Seneca's often-cited tract in which he complains about the noise emanating from the bathhouse below his apartment:

> For someone who wants seclusion to read and study . . . I'm really in trouble. . . . Just imagine the whole range of voices which can irritate my ears. When the more muscular types are exercising and swinging about lead weights in their hands, and when they are straining themselves, or at least pretending to strain, I hear groans. And when they hold their breath for a while and then let it out, I hear hissing and very hoarse gasps. . . . Now, if a ballplayer comes along and begins to count his score aloud, I'm definitely finished. . . . And then imagine people diving into the pool with a great splash of water.[11]

More noise was produced by all the eating and drinking that went on in a big bathhouse. Various snack bars and restaurants adjoined such a facility, and slaves hawked fast food inside the complex itself. Like the food vendors at modern baseball and football games, these slaves made quite a racket. According to Seneca, "I could wear myself out just listening to the variety of shouts

The large athletic field at Pompeii, located near the town's amphitheater. Smaller versions of such outside exercise facilities existed in many large Roman bathhouses.

among people selling drinks, sausages, and pastries. Each restaurant or snack bar has its own huckster with his own recognizable jingle." [12] In addition, a large bathhouse featured gift shops, gardens for strolling and leisure conversation, a small theater, and libraries and reading rooms. Combining many features of modern malls and athletic and social clubs, the *thermae* were places where people could find relaxation and entertainment for a pleasant hour or an entire day.

Chapter 2

The Art of the Dinner Party

Next to visiting the communal bath-houses, probably the most common leisure activity in ancient Rome was going out to eat. As remains the case today, this pursuit took two main forms—going to a restaurant or to someone's house for dinner. If one chose the first option, Rome and other cities and towns had numerous small cookshops or snack bars (*thermopolii*), the ancient equivalent of modern fast-food restaurants. These became widely popular during the late Republic and early Empire. Archaeologists have discovered the remains of more than two hundred of them in the city of Pompeii, which had only about twenty thousand inhabitants. There must have been several thousand such establishments in Rome because it boasted a population of close to a million in this period. One reason for the large number of cookshops was that most middle- and lower-class apartments did not have cooking facilities. Some of the apartment blocks likely had communal cooking hearths located in a central courtyard, but large numbers of city dwellers purchased cooked food at the *thermopolii* and brought it home.

Typically, such a cookshop opened directly onto the sidewalk so that customers walked right up to a wide countertop to order the food. Recessed into the countertop were one or more metal grills powered by small charcoal fires for cooking sausages and other meats. Ceramic jars kept meat that had been recently cooked warm for a while. Most of the rest of the fare at such shops

This nineteenth-century reconstruction of a street in Pompeii shows a customer at a typical snack bar with its open front and L-shaped counter.

was uncooked, including bread, cheese, figs, dates, nuts, cakes, and wine.

There were also more formal restaurants, where patrons sat at tables and could choose from a more extensive menu. But many Romans, mainly of the middle and upper classes, found it more appealing either to give or attend a private dinner party. A few of these were splendid affairs with many guests, a wide range of expensive dishes, and elaborate live entertainment. However, the majority of such gatherings were fairly small scale, featuring only a few guests and more modest food and entertainment. Many people felt that giving or attending dinner parties, small or large, was a welcome way to relax and unwind at the end of the work-day. Those who could afford it had guests over often, perhaps several times a week. One thing is certain. Both the host and the guests were expected to follow certain rules of etiquette, and society, or at least a certain social circle within it, judged them for how they comported themselves.

The Dinner Invitation

Many people were eager to land invitations to such parties, partly because the food was free and it was fun to socialize and enjoy the entertainment. Also, these gatherings, especially in richer homes, were places to meet important and influential people who might help one better his or her social position. In fact, it was often one's social position that dictated whether one would be asked to din-ner at all and how frequently. In the Roman social system of patronage, clients, who were deemed socially inferior to their patrons, de-pended on receiving dinner invitations from said patrons. This was viewed as a reward for the favors performed by the client for the patron on a weekly and sometimes daily ba-sis. A client was expected to vote as the pa-tron instructed, to show up at the patron's house in the morning and receive a list of er-rands to perform, and accompany the pa-tron on social and business calls, where the richer person's prestige might be enhanced by the presence of loyal followers.

For example, Martial describes a client named Selius who earned his dinner invita-tion by sitting in the audience at court and providing loud verbal support for his pa-tron, who was pleading a case:

Unmannerly Gluttons

In his history of Rome the fourth-century Roman historian Ammianus Marcellinus severely crit-icized people of all walks of life whom he deemed self-centered, uncultured, or corrupt. In this passage he singles out some commoners for their bad manners and what he sees as their obsession with food.

Their language is foul and senseless, very different from that in which the commons of earlier times expressed their feelings and wishes. . . . Most of these people are addicted to gluttony. Attracted by the smell of cooking and the shrill voices of the women, who scream from cock-crow [i.e., dawn] like a flock of starving peacocks, they stand about the courts on tip-toe, biting their fin-gers and waiting for the dishes to cool. Others keep their gaze fixed on some revolting mess of meat till it is ready.

When Selius spreads his net for a dinner and praises you, take him along, whether you are reciting or pleading a case. [Selius shouts] "That does it!" "A hit!" "A quick one!" "Cunning!" "Jolly good!" "Lovely!" That's what I was waiting for!" [Finally the patron says] "All right, you've got your dinner. Now hush."[13]

Martial also jokes about a client being passed over for invitations by a patron. He makes it clear that no matter how hurt or angry the client might be, the patron was always in the stronger position. "Since you dine without me so often," the client tells the patron, "I've found a way to spite you. I'm angry. You may invite me all you please, send [for me], beg [me]—'What will you do?' you say. What shall I do? I'll come."[14]

On the other hand, to refuse a dinner invitation might be seen as an insult. Describing upper-class snobs in the fourth century, the Roman historian Ammianus Marcellinus writes:

Their notion of the height of good breeding is that it is better for a stranger to kill someone's brother than to refuse an invitation to dinner. A senator feels that he has suffered a severe personal loss if a man, whom he has made up his mind after mature reflection to invite once, fails to appear.[15]

An even worse offense was to accept an invitation and not show up. "Who are you, to accept my invitation to dinner and never come?" Pliny the Younger demands in a letter to an acquaintance.

Roman diners recline on couches in a triclinium (dining room) in this engraving.

Here's your sentence and you shall pay my costs in full, no small sum either. It was all laid out, one lettuce each, three snails, two eggs, barley-cake, and wine with honey chilled with snow. . . . Instead, you chose to go [to someone else's party]. . . . You will suffer for this—I won't say how. It was a cruel trick done to spite one of us—yourself or most likely me, and possibly both of us.[16]

Pliny could have remedied the situation by sending one of his slaves to fetch a client. It was common practice in such cases for well-to-do hosts to fill the empty places this way, as the noted poet Horace attests. He recalls being called away from his own dinner table by his patron, Maecenas, to fill in for a guest who had failed to show.

Attire and Seating

For the vast majority who did accept their invitations and fully intended to go, there was little question of what to wear. By late republican times, standard polite party attire was the "dinner suit" (*vestis cenatoria* or *synthesis*), consisting of a simple tunic overlaid with a formal cloak. Usually both garments were of the same color, most often a bright one. Martial mentions a bright green dinner suit, for instance. Apparently, a few particularly fashion-conscious individuals tried to impress their guests by changing into different-colored outfits while the party was in progress. Martial describes a host changing eleven times in a single banquet, although this is almost certainly exaggerated for the sake of humor.

On arriving at the host's home, the guest removed his or her outdoor shoes (*calcei*) and put on slippers (*soleae*). Then, either the host or a servant led the guest to the dining room (*triclinium*), where the guest looked for his or her seat. In most situations, including ordinary family or

Mixing and Drinking Wine

The most common drink served at Roman dinner parties was wine. The average diner drank it sparingly during the meal but continued to drink it during the conversations or entertainment that followed. As a rule, people mixed their wine with water in a large bowl and ladled it into cups. Drinking undiluted wine was viewed as uncouth, or even barbarous, but heavy drinkers often preferred it this way since it had more alcohol content per cup. A drink called *mulsum*, made by sweetening wine with honey, was popular among the middle and upper classes; poorer folk often drank *posca*, a mixture of water and a low-quality, vinegar-like wine. Whereas the poor usually consumed their wine at room temperature, the well-to-do chilled theirs with ice (shipped in via donkeys from the nearest mountains and stored in underground pits until ready to be served). In most parts of the realm, where wine was the main drink, the best wines were aged from five to fifteen years; by contrast, in Rome's northern provinces, where Celtic and German influences were prevalent, many diners preferred beer over wine.

restaurant dining, Romans ate while sitting upright on chairs, stools, or benches, as is the rule today. At formal dinner parties, however, particularly those of the rich, it was customary to recline sideways on couches.

At formal banquets, guests were assigned to such couches according to their social status. Those blessed with higher status enjoyed the privilege of sitting closer to the host or guest of honor. The host and his relatives sat on the head couch (*imus lectus*); the more distinguished guests had the second couch (*lectus medius*); and clients and others were assigned to the last couch (*summus lectus*). The number of guests occupying these couches varied. Seven to nine was considered ideal. But it was not unusual for a host to invite fewer than seven or more than nine. When possible, many hosts avoided an even number of guests, as a common superstition held that this was unlucky.

The Food

As soon as all the guests had arrived, made their greetings, and were seated, the food began to be served. The Romans loved food, especially gourmet food (at least from the late Republic on; tastes in earlier times were apparently simpler and meals more modest). And it was not unusual for some people to spend more than they could afford on groceries. In one of his satires, Juvenal ridicules the more extreme cases—"men who live for their palate and nothing else," who ran up food bills so big that their creditors pursued them at the mar-

ketplace. "The more hopeless their [financial] straits . . . the better they dine. They'll ransack earth, air, and water for special delicacies. Cost is no object." [17]

The fare at the fancier dinner parties reflected this passion for food. Dinner (*cena*) was customarily served in three courses, collectively called *ab ovo usque ad malla* ("from the egg to the apples"). In the first course, *gustus,* the guests nibbled on appetizers, variously including lettuce, leeks, mint, mushrooms, and other raw vegetables along with olives, eggs, snails, sardines, and shellfish. The second and main course, *prima mensa,* featured cooked meats and vegetables. The most common meats were fowl (hens, geese, and other birds), fish, sows' udders, wild boar, lamb, and pork (the Romans' favorite meat). These dishes were frequently enhanced with rich sauces. The wealthier hosts sometimes imported exotic and expensive delicacies. Juvenal mentions a party where lobster was served. Other ancient authors cite such specialties as pheasant and pheasant brains, ostrich, peacocks and peacock brains, flamingo tongues, fish livers, and the eggs of eels. Finally, the third and last course, *secunda mensa,* was the dessert, most often consisting of fruit (pears, grapes, figs, and so forth), nuts, puddings, and honey cakes and other pastries.

The cooks who prepared these dishes were usually slaves. Because good cooks were much in demand, such slaves were expensive compared to farmhands, maids, and ordinary laborers. In the first century B.C., a cook cost as much as a horse, an item only a minority of Romans could afford. A cen-

A Roman Recipe

In this excerpt from her book A Taste of Ancient Rome, *a compilation of recipes inspired by those listed in ancient documents, scholar Ilaria G. Giacosa gives the following instructions for preparing a popular dessert served at many Roman dinner parties—egg pudding.*

Serves 4. 3 eggs, 3 tbs. flour, 1 ¾ cups milk, pepper to taste, 2 ½ oz. pine nuts, 1–2 tbs. raisin wine, 4 tsp. honey. Beat the eggs in a bowl with the flour and milk. Add pepper and heat in a pan. Meanwhile, grind the pine nuts with the raisin wine in a mortar. As soon as the egg mixture begins to boil, remove from the heat. Add the honey and the pine nut mixture. Resume cooking for approximately 15 minutes more over a low heat, stirring so that no lumps form. Pour into 1 large or 4 small individual bowls; add a teaspoon of honey and a pinch of pepper to each and serve.

tury later, when Pliny the Younger was entertaining, the price of a cook was equivalent to that of three horses. Finding the right cook was so important to the historian Sallust that he is said to have paid one hundred thousand sesterces, ten times the annual salary of a Roman soldier, for his.

These cooks had the benefit of many cookbooks. Gaius Matius, the son of one of Julius Caesar's close friends, wrote three—*The Cook, The Fishmonger,* and *The Pickle-Maker.* In the early first century A.D., a well-to-do man named Apicius, who was renowned as a gourmet and a glutton, wrote two books, one on cooking and one on sauces. These have not survived; but he lent his name to a popular style of cooking—*Apiciana cotura*—and one of his later admirers (probably in the fourth century) pub-

lished a cookbook under the name Apicius, which has survived. Among the many recipes listed are those for ostrich, stuffed dates, and seventeen different ways of preparing pork.

Another common custom reflecting the Romans' preoccupation with food was serving a different grade or quality of food to different dinner guests, depending on their social status and relationship with the host. Many hosts ordered that the more expensive and elaborate dishes be served to themselves and the most distinguished guests. Meanwhile, the less esteemed clients and others, especially freedmen (who ranked just above slaves), received cheaper, simpler fare, a humiliating experience described by Juvenal and other writers. The lower-ranking people might also have to make do with cheaper wine and tableware. Pliny the Younger strongly disapproved of this practice. In a letter to a friend, he describes a host whom he "happened to be dining with" who engaged in "a sort of stingy extravagance." The host and "a select few," which included Pliny, got the most appealing food while the rest received "cheap scraps." The host

> even put the wine into tiny little flasks, divided into three categories. . . . One lot was intended for himself and for us, another for his lesser friends (all of his friends are graded), and the third for his and our freedmen. My neighbor at table noticed this and asked me if I approved. I said that I did not. "So what do you do?" he asked. [I answered:] "I serve the same to everyone, for when I invite guests it is for a meal, not to make class distinctions; I have brought them as equals to the same table, so I give them the same treatment in everything." "Even freedmen?" "Of course, for then they are my fellow diners, not freedmen." [18]

Roman Table Manners

It is unclear how Pliny felt about some other eating customs of the day. He probably accepted most prevailing table manners, a number of which would appear odd or even uncouth today. Most foods were eaten with the fingers, for example. (Meats and many vegetables were precut, sliced, or chopped in the kitchen, then brought out on platters.) An exception was runny foods, such as soups, puddings, and eggs, which were eaten with a spoon.

Also, it was common for the guests to bring along their own napkins. With these they not only wiped their mouths but also wrapped up their leftovers (*apophoreta*) to take home, the Roman equivalent of a "doggy bag." Martial pokes fun at a man who had the gall to walk off with the leftovers of some of his fellow diners as well as his own. Another breach of etiquette was to steal others' napkins. The poet Catullus addressed such a fellow this way: "While we joke and drink, you lift the napkins of the careless. You think it clever? You're wrong, you fool. It's a downright dirty and vulgar trick. . . . Return my napkin, then." [19]

Among other table manners that would be frowned on today was belching. It may have been accepted among Romans as a polite gesture signifying satisfaction with the meal. Humorists like Juvenal and Martial also mention farting, spitting, and urinating into a jar. However, it seems likely that they were ridiculing a few obnoxious individuals rather than describing common practices. Similarly, another practice occasionally described by ancient writers—diners purposely inducing vomiting to make room for more food—was almost certainly not widespread. That these writers made a special effort to single out a few noted bulimics suggests that such behavior was more the exception than the rule.

One slovenly habit that was the rule at Roman dinner parties was tossing various food scraps onto the floor. These included eggshells, cherry pits, fish heads and bones, lobster shells, half-eaten chicken legs, and so forth. A number of surviving ancient mosaics show dining room floors littered with such refuse, which the host's slaves had to clean up when the party was over.

The Entertainment

In addition to the expected spread of food, those hosts who could afford it provided live entertainment. This could take many forms, depending on how much the host was willing to spend and, perhaps more importantly, on the peculiar tastes of the host and his guests. As remains true today, some party crowds were more cultured and refined whereas others were more coarse and unsophisticated.

In more cultured households, like that of Pliny the Younger, the entertainment usually consisted of music and literary readings, collectively referred to as *acroama*. Like some other wealthy men, Pliny kept slaves

Common items used by Roman cooks, including pottery mixing bowl and sauce pan, trivet (on which to rest hot containers), measuring cup, salt shaker, and serving tray.

or paid freedmen (usually educated Greeks) who were skilled in these arts. In a letter, Pliny praises his freedman Zosimus, whose "delivery is clear and intelligent, his acting correct and balanced, and he plays the lyre [harp] well. . . . He also reads speeches, his-tory, and poetry so well that it might be his sole accomplishment." [20]

Some hosts preferred to do the readings themselves, sometimes including their own poetry. Martial describes a host who sound-ly bored his guests by reciting "bulky vol-

A poet reads to a group of nobles following a meal. One young woman is so moved by his words that she is overcome with emotion.

A Host Bores His Guests

The humorist Martial penned this epigram (D.R. Shackleton Bailey's translation) chiding a host whose poetry readings bored Martial and the other guests at a dinner party.

This and no other is the reason why you invite me to dinner, Ligurinus: to recite your verses. I take my slippers off [and prepare to eat]. Immediately, a bulky volume is brought in among the lettuces and sharp [fish] sauce. Another [volume] is read through while the first course hangs fire. There's a third, and the dessert is not yet come. And you recite a fourth and finally a fifth roll. [Most ancient books consisted of long parchments rolled around a stick.] If you serve me boar this often, it stinks. But if you don't consign your damnable poems to the mackerel, Ligurinus, in future you will dine at home by yourself.

umes" of "damnable poems"[21] through all three courses of dinner. At least Pliny recognized he lacked the talent. "I am told I read badly," he wrote to the noted historian Suetonius. "I mean when I read verse, for I can manage speeches, though this seems to make my verse-reading all the worse. So, as I am planning to give an informal reading to some of my friends, I am thinking of making use of one of my freedmen."[22]

Other modes of entertainment at the more cultured parties might include an *aretalogus,* a fellow who told amusing or thought-provoking stories, often from mythology and folklore. Another similar kind of specialist was the *comoedus,* a performer who recited passages from classic drama (both tragedy and comedy). As a rule, these men entertained during the meal itself. When dinner was over, it was time for the guests to engage in polite conversation. The orator Cicero suggested some ground rules in his treatise *On Duties.* The discussion should be uncontroversial and if possible witty, he said. Also, no one speaker should "exclude all others." Rather, he "should think it fair in shared conversation, just as in other things, for everyone to have a turn." In addition:

> Conversations are for the most part about domestic business or public affairs or else the study and teaching of the arts. We should, then, even if the discussion begins to drift to other matters, make an effort to call it back to the subject.[23]

In contrast, at less-cultured parties the conversation sometimes led to arguments. These, in turn, might escalate into brawls, especially when the participants had had too much to drink. Lucian mentions two party guests getting into a fistfight over possession of some leftovers.

The guests at such parties also tended to be less interested in literary recitations; they preferred more physical kinds of entertainment, such as acrobats, dancers, actors performing slapstick skits, gladiators or wrestlers sparring, and the witty banter of jesters (*scurra*). A jester was a performer who specialized in telling off-color jokes and stories and insulting the guests, in the style of modern comics like Don Rickles. Usually, the butts of these insults accept-ed them in a spirit of good fun, but there were exceptions. At a party Lucian attended, for example, a man responded to a jester's insults by challenging him to a fight. And to everyone's surprise, the jester won!

The loser probably found it hard to live down this humiliation, as juicy news was sure to travel fast through his social circle. Of course, he could always try to worm his way into the dinner parties of another circle. On any given night, good food, drink, and entertainment could be found in private gatherings all over Rome.

Diverse Theatrical Displays

Large numbers of Romans enjoyed the theater. In ancient Rome, the term theater did not denote simply formal plays presented in theaters but also a number of other kinds of shows involving actors and other performers. These diverse theatrical displays ranged from comic skits performed on street corners and makeshift outdoor stages, to scripted plays staged in magnificent stone theaters, to balletlike presentations with music, to dramatic recitations. What is more, no single theatrical form completely superseded the others; all remained in force to one degree or another throughout the five centuries of the Roman Empire. Clearly, the Romans enjoyed and demanded a wide variety of theatrical styles. In the words of theater historian Oscar G. Brockett:

> We can probably grasp the essence of Roman theater more readily by comparing it with United States television programming, for it encompassed acrobatics, trained animals, jugglers, athletic events, music and dance, dramatic skits, short farces, and full-length dramas. The Roman public was as fickle as our own. Like channel-switchers, they frequently left one event for another and demanded diversions capable of withstanding all competition.[24]

Though never as popular as larger-scale public games like gladiatorial bouts and chariot

Patrons converse outside a Roman theater before entering to watch the play. In addition to formal plays, the Romans enjoyed a number of less formal theatrical styles.

races, the theatricals offered a pleasant diversion for Romans of all walks of life.

Impromptu Verses

The manner in which the Roman theatricals developed is still a bit sketchy. Roman society had no significant theatrical traditions of its own and erected no formal theaters until the late Republic, some seven centuries after Rome's founding. As with so many other aspects of their cultural life, the Romans borrowed many of their theatrical traditions from others. In particular, they

drew on the Greeks, who invented the art form of the theater almost overnight during the sixth and fifth centuries B.C. As the late noted classical scholar Edith Hamilton puts it:

There is hardly even a suggestion anywhere of a native [Roman] product supplanted by the imported. . . . [Perhaps the early] Roman shepherds and farmers had little inclination to spend valuable time in singing songs and making up stories. . . . A sense of poetry was not strong in the Roman people. Their natural genius did not urge them to artistic expression. . . . Later Roman critics speak of a native comedy, dramatic improvisations at festivals, but there is no warrant for supposing that it was ever written down and it had no direct literary descendants.[25]

The pre-Greek "improvisations at festivals" that Hamilton spoke of were known as Fescennine verses. The Romans borrowed them from the Etruscans, the culturally advanced people who inhabited the region north of Rome until the Etruscan cities were absorbed into the Roman commonwealth during the fourth and third centuries B.C.

The remains of the Theater of Epidaurus in southern Greece are so well preserved that plays are still presented there. The Greeks invented the art of theater and drama.

The Etruscans sang or spoke the verses, which they made up as they went along, at weddings and religious festivals. Apparently one person or group recited, after which another person or group hurled verses back. The early Romans were strongly influenced by Etruscan culture. By 500 B.C. or so, Latin versions of the Fescennine verses were common attractions at Roman festivals. The performers were called *histriones*, from which the modern term histrionic, denoting the art of acting, derives.

This wall painting showing Etruscan entertainers was found in the so-called Tomb of the Jugglers. Early Roman actors were influenced by Etruscan models.

Greek entertainers perform on a public street. The phylakes, *consisting of short comic skits, were widely popular and eventually spread to Rome.*

Farces and Mimes

In time, these informal, impromptu performances were overshadowed by new theatrical forms based on Greek models. In the late fourth century cultural influences from the Greek cities of southern Italy began to creep into the Roman-controlled lands of the peninsula's central region. Among these influences were the *phylakes*. They consisted of farces (funny shows featuring slapstick humor and improbable situations) performed in town squares and on street corners. The actors, who wore masks with exaggerated facial features, acted out a story, improvising dialogue, jokes, songs, and dances to help tell the tale.

As the Greek *phylakes* spread across Italy, the Romans adopted them and performed them in Latin, calling them Atellan farces (*fabula Atellana*). These minor theatricals are perhaps best described as short skits similar to those presented on television variety shows like *Saturday Night Live*. Each skit revolved around a simple idea or situation, such as eating too much, getting drunk, losing one's faculties in old age, an arrogant person learning humility the hard way, and so forth. Eventually, popular stock characters evolved. These included the fools and gluttons Maccus and Bucco; Pappus, a somewhat senile old fuddy-duddy; and Dossenus, a hunchback.

The Atellan farces declined considerably in popularity during late republican times, but they made a comeback during the early Empire. This was thanks largely to Augustus, who thought they were worth reviving. During this later period, people wrote down some of the better farces, but regrettably only their titles have survived. Among others, these include *The Gelded Boar, The Bride of Pappus, The Baker,* and *The Pregnant Virgin.*

The main reason for the temporary decline of the impromptu farces was the sharp rise in popularity of the mime, another early cultural import from Greece. In the third century B.C., when Rome absorbed the Greek cities of southern Italy, many Romans became fond of Greek Doric mimes. Another form of street theater, these were short comic skits similar in some ways to the *phylakes.* The dialogue was either spoken or sung, for example. (The idea of a mime actor who does not speak is a modern development.) The actors wore masks to represent stock characters. However, the mimes were more realistic, earthy, and racy, often featuring sexually obscene language and gestures. The mimes also employed specialized performers like acrobats and jugglers.

The Roman mimes retained the dirty language, earthy themes, and acrobats and jugglers found in the Greek versions. But the Romans apparently felt that the masks traditionally worn by the actors made the shows too formal and less realistic. So they discarded this convention. Roman mimes used their own facial expressions to great effect, giving their performances increased realism and a greater range of comic possibilities. Another difference between the Greek and Roman mimes was that the Roman version allowed women to play women's parts. In Greece, by contrast, women's roles were always played by men. Roman mimes came to include dancing girls who sometimes stripped, magicians, tightrope walkers, and so forth. Combining these with the skits, jokes, acrobats, and jugglers produced shows that must have resembled the American burlesque shows of the early twentieth century.

Early Roman Plays

The Romans had adopted the farces and mimes primarily from the Greek cities of Italy and Sicily. In the late third century B.C., however, Rome began to have close contact with mainland Greece and the Greek kingdoms of the eastern Mediterranean. And in the second century B.C. Rome conquered these Greek lands. As a result, many Roman soldiers, administrators, and travelers spent months and sometimes years in Greek cities, where they were heavily exposed to Greek customs and culture. This led to a new and potent surge of Roman interest in Greek theatricals.

In particular, the Romans found themselves drawn to the scripted plays they saw performed in the huge, architecturally magnificent stone theaters that existed across the Greek world. At the time, the most popular Greek theatrical style was the so-called New Comedy. Its plays featured strong, well-crafted plots in which everyday characters were thrust into and forced to deal with silly situations (in a way, the forerunners of modern situation comedies). The first known Roman version of a formal Greek play took place in about 240 B.C. when a Romanized Greek named Livius Andronicus presented two such works in Rome.

Andronicus strongly influenced the first important native Roman playwright, Gnaeus Naevius (ca. 270–ca. 201 B.C.). The titles of nine of Naevius's tragedies and thirty-four of his comedies survive; however, all

Contempt for Actors

In this excerpt from his informative book Life and Leisure in Ancient Rome, *noted scholar J.P.V.D. Balsdon provides this thumbnail sketch of the social position of Roman actors.*

Most actors and actresses were slaves or freedmen. . . . Under the Republic there certainly had been some free-born men who acted, and under the Empire there may well have been stage-struck citizens who were professional actors just as there were Roman citizens who became gladiators. . . . Any Roman who acted on the public stage was stigmatized formally, in that his name could not appear on the official list of property-owning citizens and he could not be called up for military service. . . . [A few actors made a lot of money and associated with emperors and other important people, but] the great majority led obscure, sordid lives. . . . From the surviving letters of antiquity, actors receive little but abuse and contempt, and it is easy to forget that, wherever there has been acting, there have been men and women wholeheartedly devoted to their art, artists of a very high order.

This drawing of a Roman actor was inspired by a statue.

but a few lines of these works are lost. One thing is certain: From this time on, comedy remained far more popular with Roman audiences than tragedy. The exact reasons for this are unknown. It could be that most Roman audiences lacked the education and sophistication of the Greek audiences that reveled in tragic stories with complex plots and lofty poetry.

Whatever the reasons for the Roman preference for comedy, in the second century B.C. Roman playwrights began turning out large numbers of Latin versions of Greek comedies. The Roman plays closely imitated the themes, plots, and characters of the originals, even going so far as to give most of the characters Greek names. Common Greek stock characters were simply transferred from Greek to Roman stages. These included conceited soldiers, stupid old men, prostitutes, social parasites, and mischievous slaves and their easily fooled masters.

Of these characters, the most popular by far was the clever slave who enjoyed outwitting his master. Slavery was a major and deeply ingrained institution in Rome, where nearly every family except the very poorest had at least one or two slaves. So it is not surprising that slaves played such important roles in Roman plays. In fact, more often than not, the clever slave was the leading character, "the only one with brains," Hamilton remarks, "who succeeds in fooling all of the people all of the time." [26]

A Slave Tries to Avoid Trouble

The main characters in many of Plautus's plays are slaves. For the most part, they either cleverly outwit or cringe in fear of their masters (or both), two situations Roman audiences found amusing. This example of a cringing slave is from E.F. Watling's translation of Plautus's The Ghost.

The way to be a useful slave is to be afraid of trouble even when you've done no wrong. The ones who are not afraid of anything even when they *have* deserved trouble, are going the right way to *get* trouble. They may train for the cross-country [i.e., an escape] . . . and when they get caught, what have they done? They've simply doubled their trouble—which is more than they can ever do with their money. . . . The way I go about it is to see that if anyone gets into trouble it isn't me. I like to keep my skin the way it's always been—whole, and not beaten more than I care for. As long as I keep a watch on myself like that, I'll always have a roof over my head; trouble can rain on other people, not on me.

Plautus (left) and Terence were the leading playwrights of early Roman theater. Both based their plays to a large extent on existing Greek comedies.

One Greek convention the Romans did not adopt in their formal plays was the use of masks, which had been a mainstay of the New Comedy as well as of Greek tragedy. As in mimes, the actors in Roman plays relied on their facial expressions to convey mood and emotion. This allowed them to develop and perfect their acting skills to a high degree, perhaps higher than that achieved by masked Greek actors.

A second Greek theatrical convention the Romans did not yet adopt was the theaters themselves. Roman plays continued to be presented on makeshift wooden stages that could be erected almost anywhere in less than a day. The largest versions were probably about five to eight feet high and fifty to sixty feet wide. Behind the acting platform, or *pulpitum*, stood a wooden wall called the *scaenae frons*, which was perhaps twelve feet high. The actors made their exits and entrances through doors cut into this wall, and city and country scenes may have been painted on it to provide a simple but effective setting.

Plautus and Terence

The men who wrote the plays that were performed on these stages generally came from the fringes of polite society. Most appear to have been former slaves, foreigners, or the sons of poor farmers. From the latter group emerged the first of the two leading Roman playwrights of the age—Titus Maccius

Plautus (ca. 254–184 B.C.). After working for a while as a stage carpenter and probably an actor, Plautus began writing plays in the style of the Greek New Comedy. He may have written as many as 130 plays, but all but 20 of them are lost. Three of the most famous and beloved are *The Pot of Gold*, about an old miser who worries that his gold will be stolen; *Milos Gloriosus* (or *The Braggart Warrior*), in which an arrogant soldier is exposed as the fool that he is; and *The Twin Menaechmi,* about twins separated at birth and later reunited under confusing and hilarious circumstances.

These works are clearly not near carbon copies of Greek originals, as a majority of Roman comedies of the day seem to have been. According to J.P.V.D. Balsdon, Plautus offered a fresh, inventive approach, taking

> great liberties with the Greek originals . . . cutting some passages [and] expanding on others, so as to give them a Roman complexion. And he made great fun of the Latin language itself. To read, every one of his plots is extremely funny, and the plots of more than one of them have a universality of appeal which has given them a permanence in literature.[27]

Plautus supplied not only funny plots but also a stream of jokes and slapstick antics that were guaranteed to please his audiences. Since much of his humor was vulgar, as in the mimes, these crowds were likely drawn mainly from the middle and lower classes.

The other master of Roman comedy was Publius Terentius Afer, known as Terence (ca. 185–ca. 159 B.C.). Most of the details of his life are unknown, other than that he was born a slave in Carthage (in North Africa) and was brought to Rome as a young man by a Roman senator who educated and freed him. Terence wrote only six plays, all of which, fortunately, have survived. They are *The Girl from Andros, The Mother-in-Law, Self-Tormentor, The Eunuch, The Brothers,* and *Phormio.*

Terence followed Greek originals more closely than Plautus and aimed his plays more at the upper, more educated classes. Thus, Terence's works have less slapstick and bawdy humor, more realistic situations, and more natural dialogue. His style is best described as charming, full of wisdom about life and human nature, and often refreshingly honest. He readily admits, for example, that playwrights and other artists constantly borrow from their predecessors. If the playwright "is not allowed to make use of the same characters as other writers," he states in *The Eunuch,*

> how can he still bring on a running slave, virtuous wives and dishonest courtesans [prostitutes], greedy spongers and braggart soldiers? How can he show . . . deception of an old man by his slave, love, hatred, and suspicion? Nothing in fact is ever said which has not been said before.[28]

Theaters and Theatricals of the Empire

Formal written plays continued to be performed in the centuries following Plautus and

These panels depict Roman actors cavorting on the stage. Eventually, mimes and Atellan farces were presented on stages along with scripted plays.

Terence. Over time, some of the makeshift, temporary stages on which they were presented became quite large and elaborate. One mentioned in the ancient sources accommodated as many as eighty thousand spectators and was decorated with statues and tapestries. The need for permanent theaters was now plain. In 55 B.C. the first stone theater in Rome, the Theater of Pompey, was erected. Its shape was a hemisphere (like half of a pie), and its seating section ran along the curved wall. On the inside of the straight wall, behind the stage, loomed the *scaenae frons,* which was sumptuously decorated with columns, statues, and other finery. The structure sat about eight thousand people. A larger theater, the Theater of Marcellus, which opened in Rome in 11 B.C., sat fourteen thousand people. And over the next two centuries, roughly 125 other permanent theaters appeared across the Empire.

But though these facilities were never empty, the demand for formal, scripted plays declined somewhat in the last century of the Republic and the first century of the Empire. This was partly because mimes, and perhaps Atellan farces as well, began to be presented in theaters. These traditional theatricals no doubt offered stiff competition for the plays.

More influential in the partial decline of formal plays was the tremendous rise in popularity of public games such as gladiatorial fights, chariot races, and wild beast shows. These, as well as violent sporting events like boxing, had already begun to compete with plays and other theatricals as early as Terence's day. In the prologue of his play *The Mother-in-Law,* he tells how his first and second attempts to stage the play were unsuccessful because the spectators were expecting to see boxers and gladiators:

I have never been able to gain a hearing uninterrupted [for this play]. . . . At the first production, much talk of some boxers, as well as the rumor that a tight-rope walker would appear . . . forced me off the stage. . . . I then decided to . . . put it on a second time. The first part was doing well when news arrived that there was to be a gladiators' show. In surged the people, pushing, shouting, jostling for a place, leaving me powerless to hold my own.[29]

Also competing with stage plays for the attention of Roman audiences was a newer theatrical form that developed in the early Empire—the pantomimes (*fabula saltica*). These consisted of ballet-like shows in which a solo dancer (the *pantomimus*) used elegant footwork and bodily gestures to act out a story. Usually, the dancer played all the parts, indicating the different characters by changing masks. Some pantomimes, however, featured multiple dancers. The performers, who were

Terence Pleads with His Audience

For his third attempt to stage The Mother-in-Law, *which proved successful, Terence provided a prologue that recapped the reasons that the previous attempts had failed. This excerpt is from Betty Radice's translation of the play.*

Now for my sake give a fair hearing to my plea. Once more I am presenting *The Mother-in-Law*, a play for which I have never been able to gain a hearing uninterrupted, so much as misfortune dogged its progress. You can remedy this by your understanding, if you will support our efforts. At the first production, much talk of some boxers, as well as the rumor that a tight-rope walker would appear, the mob of their supporters, shouting, and women's screaming forced me off the stage before the end. I then decided to . . . put it on a second time. The first part was doing well when news arrived that there was to be a gladiators' show. In surged the people, pushing, shouting, jostling for a place, leaving me powerless to hold my own. Today there is no distraction, all is calm and peaceful; this is my chance to present the play and your opportunity to do honor to the stage. Do not be responsible for allowing the art of drama to sink into the hands of a few. . . . Grant my plea on behalf of the author. . . . Do not let him be cheated and derided by unjust men. For my sake . . . listen in silence. Others will then feel encouraged to write [plays], and it will be profitable for me in the future to present new plays bought at my own expense.

These Roman theatrical masks were found at Pompeii. The city of twenty thousand inhabitants had two theaters.

both male and female, were accompanied by musicians and singers (sometimes soloists, other times entire choirs). Most of the stories came from Greek mythology, including the creation of the world by the gods and the Trojan War, or from Greek tragedy. A few were taken from history. One of these, for instance, was titled *Cleopatra.* In his novel *The Golden Ass,* the Roman writer Apuleius includes a detailed description of a pantomime in which Venus, goddess of love, played a key role. "Venus becomingly took the center of the stage . . . and smiled sweetly," he writes.

She was surrounded by a throng of the happiest children; you would have sworn that [they] . . . were genuine Cupids who had just flown in from sky or sea. . . . Venus still more affectingly began gently to stir herself; with gradual, lingering steps, restrained swaying of the hips, and slow inclination [tilting] of the head, she began to advance, her refined movements matching the soft sounds of the flutes. Occasionally her eyes alone would dance, as at one moment she gently lowered her lids, at another imperiously signaled with threatening glances.[30]

Another kind of theatrical presentation that appeared during the early Empire was the "tragic recitation." It consisted of verses spoken and sung by actors who were accompanied by musicians and singers. These works, including several tragedies by Seneca (among them *Medea, Phaedra,* and *Oedipus*), were composed mainly for educated members of the upper classes. And because they did not even try to compete with the mimes, pantomimes, and other theatricals, they drew small audiences. Pliny the Younger, who was among the more devoted fans of the genre, wrote, "I am glad to see that literature flourishes and there is a show of budding talent, in spite of the fact that people are slow to form an audience."[31] Taken as a whole, though, Roman theatricals had no trouble attracting audiences and remained a popular leisure pursuit until the last years of the Roman Empire.

Roman Tastes in Literature

Some Romans whiled away a proportion of their leisure hours reading literature, at least from the second century B.C. on. Before this, very few Romans enjoyed literature, for two reasons. First, during Rome's early centuries the vast majority of people were illiterate and there were no libraries and few books. Only a few slaves could read, and most of them were foreigners, especially Greeks, who had been captured in war. But among native Romans, only upper-class families could afford to educate their children, and most schooling was designed to further the political or legal careers of socially prominent young men.

Second, there was no collected body of Roman literature for these early literate Romans to pursue. Mostly, their reading consisted of official election records, lists of laws, political slogans, lists of major events recorded by priests, religious hymns and chants, business inventories and ship manifests, and personal letters. There was no Roman poetry to speak of, no historical texts, no formal plays, no biographies, no novels, no philosophical or scientific treatises, and no published journals or collections of letters.

Indeed, when Roman literature finally emerged, it did so rather suddenly and blossomed quickly. Moreover, because the early writers had no significant Latin precedents to build on, they turned for inspiration to the rich, diverse literature of the Greeks. "No other great national literature goes back to an origin borrowed in all respects," Edith Hamilton writes.

In Greece the development [of literature] was the natural one, from songs and stories handed down by word of mouth and added to through unknown ages. There was a spontaneous desire in the people—farmers, shepherds, fighting men—for imaginative expression, which ultimately took literary shape and was preserved. With the Romans, it was the other way around. The literary shape came first, across the sea, from Greece. The desire for expression was secondary, following upon the discovery of an appropriate form ready-made to hand. [32]

Once Latin literature began to be produced in measurable quantity and quality, it helped create more demand for literacy, and a larger reading public rapidly developed. In the absence of statistics and other solid evidence, the extent of Roman literacy is difficult to estimate. But certain clues

The Theater of Dionysus in Athens. Just as Greek theater inspired Roman theater, Greek literature, including poetry, history, and novels, inspired Roman versions.

suggest that by the first century B.C. a majority of Romans could read. Tomb inscriptions "were set up by rich and poor alike," scholar R.H. Barrow points out. "And there is little point in an artisan putting up an epitaph if relations were incapable of reading it. The election posters placarded on the walls of Pompeii, shops signs, and public notices all imply a public which could read."[33]

Other evidence shows not only that a majority of Romans could read but also that a strong appreciation of and desire to read literature developed. By the mid–first century B.C. the book trade was flourishing, and the public eagerly awaited each new installment of the personal journal Julius Caesar kept during his conquest of Gaul. Only a few years later, following the fall of the Republic, Rome enjoyed its golden literary age, often referred to as the Augustan age of literature because the first emperor, Augustus, encouraged and patronized writers. This fertile period produced Virgil's immortal epic poetry; Horace's and Ovid's witty, timeless verses; and Livy's monumental history, now listed among the great works of world literature. Many important and talented Roman and Romanized Greek writers followed, while libraries sprang up across the Roman world. And the easy availability of books of literature gave large numbers of people one of their most enjoyable leisure outlets.

Nostalgia for Country Life

Some idea of the tastes of Roman readers can be deduced from the kinds of literature that were most prevalent and therefore likely most popular. Certainly, large numbers of Romans liked poetry. The works of major poets, such as Virgil and Horace, were taught in schools, and publication of various kinds of poetry was widespread from the late first century B.C. on.

Of these different styles of poetry, most of which copied Greek forms, pastoral verse (in several styles and meters) was a favorite, partly because it drew on and glorified traditional Roman values. Though most of the reading public lived in the cities, the Romans had always been a rustic farming people. And people of all walks of life harbored strong attachments to and nostalgia for the countryside. As a result, they enjoyed verses about simple, uncorrupted farmers, shepherds, and other country folk and the innate virtues of living and loving in the fields, forests, hills, and so forth.

On the whole, these visions of country life were highly idealized. Usually they were penned by men who, thanks to their patrons (wealthy individuals who subsidized them), did not have to work and lived comfortable lives in townhouses and country villas. These chosen few ignored the reality that simple farmers and herdsmen did backbreaking work from sunup to sundown for few material rewards. Nevertheless, such poems tapped into a deep recess of the Roman psyche and were always popular.

The most famous pastoral verses were probably the ten *Eclogues* of the Augustan writer Virgil (Publius Vergilius Maro), widely recognized as Rome's greatest poet. However, many other poets contributed to the genre. The Augustan writer Albius

An engraving depicts a Roman farming villa, with its bevy of barnyard animals. The Romans had a deep appreciation for poetry about pastoral life.

Tibullus, for instance, waxes eloquent about the virtues of the countryside in this selection from his *Elegies:*

> May I be content to live on a little [farm on a small plot of land and] . . . to avoid the summer's heat under the shade of a tree upon the bank of a flowing stream. And let me not think it shameful to hold a hoe once in a while or to urge the slow oxen with a whip. . . . When the time is right, let me tend the young vines and the large fruit trees with a farmer's deft touch. [34]

Love, Romance, and Passion

No less appealing to Roman readers was love poetry. It developed from Greek elegiac poetry, a literary form used mainly to express personal emotions and sentiments. The Greek elegy encompassed laments and epitaphs for the dead and personal reflections on life as well as love poems. Roman writers developed a special, distinctive type of love-elegy consisting of a series of verses, published over the course of months or years, that revealed a poet's romantic involvement with a woman. She was usually

Lovers Secretly Communicate

In this witty tract from his Amores (Love Affairs, *translated by Jo-Ann Shelton in her* As the Romans Did), *the Augustan poet Ovid arranges with his mistress to engage in some subtle, secret interactions at a dinner party that he, she, and her husband will be attending.*

So your husband will be attending the same banquet as us! I hope it will be his last supper! Am I supposed to act like a mere guest toward the woman I love? . . . I am not a wild animal, but I can scarcely keep my hands off you. Well then, pay attention and learn what you must do. . . . When your husband takes his place on the dining couch, put on an appearance of great innocence, and go, as a faithful wife, to lie down beside him. But as you pass, touch my foot without anyone's noticing. Watch me carefully, look for my nods and facial expressions. Figure out those secret unspoken messages and send me some of your own. Without speaking a word, I will tell you things by raising my eyebrows. You will read notes marked out by my fingers which are wet with wine. When memories of our lovemaking fill your mind, put your delicate finger on your rosy cheek. . . . When you are praying that some disaster befall your husband (he deserves it), touch the table with your hand.

his mistress. Thus, many Roman readers avidly followed the amorous relationships between Tibullus and his Delia, Ovid and Corinna, Gaius Catullus and Lesbia, and Sextus Propertius and Cynthia.

Ovid (Publius Ovidius Naso) is generally considered the master of Roman love poetry. His verses in this genre are usually filled with wry wit, charm, bittersweet observations about life, and sometimes overt references to sexual passion. Consider this delightful example from the second book of his *Amores:*

Offered a sexless heaven, I'd say *No Thank you*—women are such sweet hell. Of course one gets bored, and passion cools, but always desire begins to spiral again. Like a horse bolting, with helpless rider tugging at the reins . . . Cupid's erratic air-stream hits me, announcing love's target practice. Then shoot, boy! I can't resist you. Your aim strikes home in my heart. . . . I pity the man whose idea of bliss is eight hours' sleep. [35]

More serious and sensual is this beautiful verse by Propertius:

O let us love until we are each other—we on whom Fate these few swift hours has smiled. It will not be for long. A night will take us which must refuse to brighten into dawn. Strain closer to me, lock me in a nearness that will not fail when time would have it gone. . . . Given all your kisses, still I'd have too few. . . . O Cynthia, you and I are lovers blessed and hopeful, but who knows what day may see that last door shut? [36]

Humor

The Roman masses also enjoyed humorous poems, especially the satirical kind. Roman satire evoked laughter by criticizing, ridiculing, or lampooning various aspects of everyday life. One of the masters of the genre was Juvenal (Decimus Junius Juvenalis), whose sixteen satires were published in the early second century A.D. His relentlessly biting invective harps on the ills of a society he feels is filled with greedy, unscrupulous, corrupt, and unsavory people, particularly city dwellers; and he consistently yearns for the "good old days" when honesty, virtue, and chastity supposedly reigned. "Any place is better to live in than Rome," he complains in his third satire.

> "At Rome," said my friend, "corruption reigns supreme. The honest man is doomed to failure. And so, I am leaving my native city before I grow too old, abandoning it to corrupt, successful people, who are catapulted from insignificance to greatness by luck. Only lying, hypocrisy, crime, and blackmail succeed in Rome. . . . It is hopeless for the poor man to advance himself. The cost of living is great and standards are high. . . . Money rules all." [37]

Another of Juvenal's friends was also a popular humorist—Martial (Marcus Valerius Martialis), master of the epigram. An epigram is a short, usually witty poem expressing a specific idea, thought, or observation. The form was so popular that many prominent Roman men, poets and nonpoets alike, wrote epigrams as a sort of leisure hobby. Few compared in wit and none in sheer volume to Martial's, which make penetrating observations about every conceivable subject. In this one, he expresses pride in his

A fanciful depiction of Juvenal drawn for an eighteenth-century version of his satires.

own success as a writer: "My Rome praises my little books, loves them, recites them; I am in every pocket, every hand. Look, someone turns red, turns pale [with anger], is dazed, yawns, is disgusted. This I want. Now my poems please me."[38] Another epigram comments on greedy relatives eagerly waiting for a wealthy old man to pass on: "You are rich, Gaurus, and old. [Those] who give you presents say to you, if you have any wit to understand, 'Die.'"[39] On longing to escape the city and annoying neighbors, Martial writes, "Linus, you ask what I get out of my land near Nomentum. This is what I get out of the land: I don't see you, Linus."[40] And still another epigram muses about the absurd aspects of war: "While fleeing from the enemy, Fannius killed himself. I ask, is it not madness, dying to avoid death?"[41]

Epic Poetry and History

All of these verse forms were relatively short. But the Romans liked epic, or book-length, poetry, too. The magnificent *Iliad* (about an episode in the Trojan War) and *Odyssey* (chronicling the later adventures of one of the war's heroes), both by the eighth-century B.C. Greek bard Homer, had long before set the standard in the genre. For centuries, the Romans had admired these epics, which at first they knew in oral form, probably in abbreviated versions roughly translated into Latin. Then, in the late third century B.C., Livius Andronicus, the writer who presented the first Latin version of a Greek play in Rome, translated Homer's *Odyssey* into Latin. This inspired

the Roman playwright Naevius to create the first original Latin epic poem, *The Punic War* (about a major conflict between Rome and Carthage).

In turn, Naevius's work, along with Homer's works and some later Roman epics, had a strong influence on Virgil. His *Aeneid,* the greatest of all Roman poems, recounts the mythological tale of the founding of the Roman race in Italy by Aeneas, a Trojan prince who had escaped the burning Troy when the Greeks had sacked the city. Virgil's epic became so widely revered and beloved that thereafter the Romans proudly viewed it as their national epic.

In ancient times, the epics of Homer, Naevius, Virgil, and others, though obviously highly dramatized and romanticized, were also seen as historical works of a kind. So, bridging the gap between these and true histories, like the massive chronicle of Rome's saga penned by Livy (Titus Livius), was partly accomplished by switching from verse to prose. As Barrow points out, "To the Romans, epic is . . . the epic of Rome; Rome is the heroine inspiring Romans to heroic deeds to fulfill her destiny. On exactly the same level is history, for such a history as Livy's . . . is simply prose epic."[42]

The first Roman history written in Latin (of which only a few fragments survive) was that of the noted senator Cato the Elder during the mid–second century B.C. Cato inspired a new generation of Latin historians who became known as the "annalists" because they consulted the *Annales Maximi,* lists of crucial events long kept by Rome's chief priests. However, these and

Aeneas carries his aged father Anchises from the burning Troy in this eighteenth-century engraving. Beloved by the Romans, the Aeneid *remains popular today.*

most later Roman historians, including Livy, were less interested in historical accuracy and more in providing moral instruction to their readers. Very few tried to verify the information in their sources, and most freely included hearsay and paraphrased or even fabricated speeches. Livy wanted his audience to "trace the process of our moral decline," as he put it in the introduction to his masterwork, the *History of Rome from Its Foundation,*

> to watch, first, the sinking of the foundations of morality . . . and the dark dawning of our modern day when we

can neither endure our vices nor face the remedies needed to cure them. The study of history is the best medicine for a sick mind; for in history . . . you can find for yourself and your country both examples and warnings; fine things to take as models, [and] base things, rotten through and through, to avoid.[43]

Biography and Autobiography

The next great Roman historian after Livy was Publius Cornelius Tacitus, whose *Annals*

Virgil's Tragic Heroine Rages

This magnificent, impassioned speech from Virgil's great epic poem the Aeneid *(Patric Dickinson's translation) is delivered by Dido, the queen of Carthage. When the Trojan hero Aeneas landed in her country on his way to Italy, she fell in love with him; now that he is about to continue his journey, she is overcome with anger.*

You traitor! Did you hope to mask such treachery and silently slink from my land? Is there nothing to keep you? Nothing that my life or our love has given you, knowing that if you go, I cannot but die? . . . Why, if Troy still stood, would you seek Troy across these ravening waters? Is it unknown lands and unknown homes you seek, or is it from me you flee? You see me weep. I have nothing else but tears and your right hand to plead with. . . . If you ever found in me any sort of sweetness, pity me now! . . . If prayer has any potency [strength] change your mind! . . . [When he refuses to listen:] Oh God, I am driven raving mad with fury! . . . Go! Seek Italy on a tempest, seek your realms over the storm-crests, and I pray if the gods are as true to themselves as their powers that you will be smashed on the rocks, calling on Dido's name!

Dido, queen of Carthage, dies after her lover Aeneas abandons her.

and *Histories* fascinated literate people across the Roman Empire during the late first and early second centuries A.D. Tacitus's writing is more concise and generally more critical and powerful than Livy's, though not as entertaining. In addition, Tacitus's work has a biographical feel, as he tends to cover the history of an era by focusing on the lives and deeds of a few of its major historical figures. In fact, another of his works, the *Agricola* (about his father-in-law, a noted military general), is a purposeful combination of history and biography.

A number of other writers, both before and after Tacitus, wrote biographical works. The most important was Plutarch, a Romanized Greek of the first century A.D. His fifty biographies of noted Greek and Roman leaders were written to demonstrate to his fellow Greeks that the Romans were more fit than the Greeks to rule the world. He also wanted to remind the Romans that Greece had once produced soldiers and statesmen as great as Rome's. The title of the work—*Parallel Lives*—derived from Plutarch's unusual format, in which he did many of the biographies in pairs. Each pair includes a study of a well-known Greek and an equally famous Roman whose character and deeds were to some degree similar.

Many Romans also tried their hand at autobiography. In the first century B.C., for example, several Roman politicians and generals recorded their own lives and exploits. The best-known example is Julius Caesar's *Commentaries,* one covering his campaigns in Gaul, the other his victories in the civil war that soon followed. During the Empire,

This portrait of Plutarch is fanciful. No one knows what he looked like.

some emperors and their relatives also wrote autobiographies. Only one of these works has survived: the *Res gestae* of Augustus, a brief and rather dry overview of his major achievements.

Letters and Novels

Another kind of popular literature avidly absorbed by Roman readers consisted of published collections of the letters of noted individuals. Some of these letters were not originally written for publication. The greatest surviving collection of all, for example, that of the orator Cicero, was collected and published following his death. In contrast,

Tacitus Combines History and Biography

This excerpt from Tacitus's Agricola *helps set the scene for Gnaeus Julius Agricola's assumption of the governorship of the recently established Roman province of Britannia and his expansion of that province through conquest. It also illustrates the concise, direct prose style and moralistic tone for which Tacitus is famous and widely admired.*

Neither before nor since has Britain ever been in a more disturbed and perilous state. Veterans had been massacred, colonies burned to the ground, armies cut off. They had to fight for their lives before they could think of victory. The campaign, of course, was conducted under the direction and leadership of another—the commander of whom belonged the decisive success and the credit for recovering Britain. Yet everything combined to give the young Agricola fresh skill, experience, and ambition; and his spirit was possessed by a passion for military glory—a thankless passion in an age in which a sinister construction was put upon distinction and a great reputation was as dangerous as a bad one.

Pliny the Younger did compose many of his letters with publication in mind. "I have now made a collection," he says in one of them. "I shall set about recovering any letters which have hitherto been put away and forgotten, and I shall not suppress any which I may write in the future."[44] As for why so many ordinary Romans would want to read the letters of Pliny, Cicero, and other famous men, one need only consider how eager modern readers are to know what goes on in the private domains of the rich and powerful.

The form of still another popular Roman literary genre, the novel, was based on Greek models. Ancient novels were usually long prose narratives telling fictional stories, almost always colorful and romantic in tone.

The first known major Latin novel was the *Satyricon* by the first-century A.D. writer Petronius, sections of which survive. Only a single Roman novel has come down through the ages complete—*The Golden Ass.* Written during the second century A.D. by Lucius Apuleius, a Roman writer born in North Africa, it concerns a young man (also named Lucius) who, through black magic, is turned into an ass. After a series of adventures, he encounters the kindly goddess Isis, who transforms him back into a person. It is a shame that other Latin novels have not survived. If the *Satyricon* and *Golden Ass* are representative of the genre, it is not difficult to see why so many Romans enjoyed reading literature.

Games and
Sporting Activities

S ome people express surprise on discovering that the Romans enjoyed many of the same leisure games and sporting activities that are widely popular today. These include ball games, gambling, board games, hunting, fishing, mountain climbing, swimming, boating, boxing, and others. In truth, it would be surprising if the Romans had not indulged in most of these activities because the modern Western world inherited them from the ancient Greeks and Romans.

Indeed, it is essential to bring the Greeks into any discussion of the informal games and sports pursued by the Romans. Rome had increasing contact with Greek culture from the early third century B.C. on. And after the second century B.C., when Rome con-

quered the Greek lands, large sectors of the Roman world were largely inhabited by Greeks, many of whom became Roman citizens. (All became citizens in A.D. 212 per a decree of the emperor Caracalla.) Over the course of many centuries, therefore, the highly imitative Romans absorbed numerous elements of Greek culture, including many aspects of leisure life.

Ball Games

Still, some games and sports surely developed independently in both the Greek and Roman spheres. One leisure activity that likely arose independently and very early in the societies of both Rome and Greece (as well as in other societies around the world) was playing ball. Most often, people in the

63

Romans play a ball game in this scene from a wall painting. The game depicted here may be the one described by the Greek doctor Galen.

Roman world engaged in ball games in city streets or in country fields, as they do today; but bathhouses, gymnasiums, private clubs, and even some private homes also witnessed friendly ball games on a regular basis.

Most of these games utilized one of three basic kinds of balls. There was a small hard ball, the *harpastum,* probably a slightly larger version of a modern golf ball. A second kind of ball, the *pila,* was a bit bigger than a *harpastum* and was also softer, as it was stuffed with feathers. The third type of ball in common use was called a *follis.* It consisted of an animal bladder (or perhaps sometimes a leather pouch) filled with air, so it may have resembled a modern bas-

ketball. Martial calls the *follis* the ball of choice for children and old people, though others used it too in certain games.

There were numerous games involving these balls, some of them team sports, the others pitting one individual against another. Very little information, however, has survived about how they were played. One popular one mentioned by several ancient writers—*trigon*—utilized a small hard ball. The ball itself was often called a *trigon,* and it was likely a version of the *harpastum.* As roughly reconstructed by modern scholars, three players stood, as if on the points of a triangle, facing one another. As play commenced, they threw one or more balls back and forth, usually as hard and fast as possible. The object was twofold—to complete as many catches as possible and to cause the other players to drop the ball or balls. Meanwhile, a scorer kept track of the missed balls, and whoever ended up with the lowest score was the winner. This is the game that the rich former slave Trimalchio plays in a bathhouse in a scene in Petronius's novel the *Satyricon*. "Suddenly," the narrator recalls,

> we saw a bald old man in a reddish shirt, playing ball with some long-haired boys. . . . He was taking his

Exercise and Good Fun Combined

In this excerpt from his treatise titled Exercise with a Small Ball, *the Greek physician Galen, who became Rome's foremost medical practitioner, describes a ball game that was apparently similar to modern "keep away," except that the player could wrestle the ball from an opponent.*

[The game] is the only one which is so democratic that anyone, no matter how small his income, can take part. You need no nets, no weapons, no horses, no hounds—just a single ball, and a small one at that. . . . The capacity . . . to move all the parts of the body equally . . . is something found in no other exercise except that with a small ball. . . . When for example, people face each other, vigorously attempting to prevent each another from taking the space between, the exercise is a very heavy, vigorous one, involving much use of the hold by the neck, and many wrestling holds. . . . The loins and legs are also subject to great strain in this kind of activity; it requires great steadiness on one's feet.

Three young Roman men play handball. Note their hand gear.

exercise in slippers and throwing a green ball around. But he didn't pick it up when it touched the ground; instead, there was a slave holding a bagful [of balls], and he supplied them to the players. . . . [Another slave] counted the balls, not those flying from hand to hand according to the rules, but those that fell to the ground. [45]

Among the other popular ball games, the famous second-century doctor Galen mentions one that appears to have been a rougher version of "keep away," a staple of many modern junior high schools. He gives a detailed account of the game in one of his treatises, saying that it was an excellent way to stay in shape. There were also team games that were likely similar to modern rugby and field hockey. Also, many Romans enjoyed games similar to modern handball or racquetball, in which they bounced a ball against a wall. Most bathhouses featured courts for these activities. And well-to-do individuals like Pliny the Younger had their own private courts in their villas. "Over the dressing room," he writes to a friend, describing his spacious mansion in Tuscany, "is built a ball court, and this is large enough for several sets of players to take different kinds of exercise." [46]

Parlor Games and Gambling

For those who preferred to spend a less strenuous hour or two of leisure time, there were numerous small-scale games that could be played in houses, on street corners, in bathhouses, or almost anywhere. One of the more common, especially among children and women, was knucklebones (*tali*), versions of which are still popular today in many corners of the globe. The four-sided playing pieces, also called *tali,* consisted of small goat or sheep bones or sometimes stone, metal, or ivory versions of them. The player tossed four at a time into the air and tried to catch them on the back of her or his hand. Sometimes the players kept score, awarding points for the number of pieces caught as well as for the way they landed.

Board games were also played in all manner of settings, from living rooms to town squares. One popular game, *Duodecim Scripta,* utilized a board with twenty-four squares set in two rows, with the squares in the bottom row numbered 1 to 12 and those in the top row marked 13 to 24 and running in the opposite direction (so that square 24 was directly above square 1). "Each player had fifteen pieces," J.P.V.D. Balsdon explains, white ones versus black ones,

and moves were determined by the throwing of three dice. At the start of the game, the white pieces were on square 1 and moved forward, the black on square 24, moving backwards. The winner was the first player who succeeded in moving all his pieces from square 1 to square 24, or from square 24 to square 1. . . . If one enemy piece was on the square to which your throw took you, it was driven back to base. [47]

Among the other popular board games was a complex war game in which the playing pieces were called "soldiers" or "robbers."

Tabula

In early Roman antiquity the game was originally known as *alea*, meaning "gambling." It soon came to be called *tabula* since it was played on a board or table. The game was popular with Roman soldiers and they spread it throughout the Mediterranean world. *Tabula* spawned a series of similar games throughout Europe and the Middle East. Our modern day game backgammon is descended from *tabula*.

The Playing Pieces and Dice

The Board

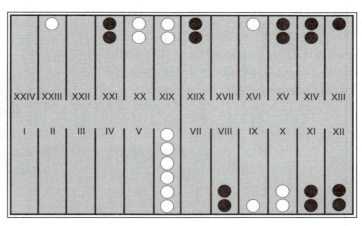

The Rules of *Tabula*

1. The board can be a backgammon board like the one illustrated above. Each player has 15 playing tokens.
2. Each token enters from square I and proceeds counterclockwise to square XXIV where it can be exited off the board and safe at "home."
3. A player throws 3 dice and these three numbers allow the player to move between 1 and 3 tokens.
4. Any part of a throw that cannot be used is lost but a player must use the whole value of his dice throw wherever possible.
5. If a player lands his token on a point with one enemy token the enemy token is removed from the board and must renter the board on square I on the next throw.
6. If a player has 2 or more tokens on a point, that position is closed to the enemy and they cannot be captured.
7. No player may move a token into the second half of the board until all tokens have entered the board.
8. A player may not exit the board with his tokens until all his tokens have entered the last quarter (squares XVIII–XXIV). This means that if a single token is hit by an enemy token, the remaining tokens are unable to move in the last quarter until he reenters the board and proceeds to the last quarter.

It must have resembled chess in some ways; the players moved their pieces from square to square in almost the exact manner as chess pawns and queens. The object was to capture all of the enemy's pieces. Noted scholar Jo-Ann Shelton describes still another widely played board game that is less well understood:

> Six Latin words were inscribed on a board or tabletop. Each word consisted of six letters, and the words were so arranged that there were eighteen letters on each side of the board. Perhaps each player had a gaming piece which he moved from letter to letter, but we have no idea how the game was played. [48]

No doubt people sometimes placed bets on these and other leisure games. Certainly the line between friendly play and gambling has always been thin and easy to cross, and gambling was rampant in ancient Roman society. Laws were passed from time to time in an effort to stop or at least control it, but they were largely ignored and almost never enforced. During century after century, people wagered large amounts of cash on games and sporting events of all kinds (with some of the bigger bets placed on the outcomes of chariot races and gladiatorial fights).

In addition to betting on the outcomes of various games and events, gamblers played dice games, some of which have survived, either intact or somewhat modified, to the present. One of these games used the *tali* from knucklebones as dice. According to Waldo E. Sweet, an authority on ancient games and sports:

> The player threw four of these dice; with four sides, there were thirty-five possible throws. The highest score, called the

Roman Street Games

In addition to knucklebones, betting on sporting events, and playing dice, the Romans engaged in various street games that might or might not involve wagers. In one, called "heads or tails" (*capita et navia*), still played today around the world, the players had to guess about the outcomes of coin tosses. In another game, "odd or even" (*par impar*), a player hid some pebbles, nuts, or other tokens in his hand and his opponent had to guess how many he held. Still another common Roman game, *micatio* (still played in southern Italy) was a variation of odd or even. It was played by two people who kept raising random numbers of fingers. Each had to guess how many the other was going to raise and the winner was the one who first guessed right.

Two Roman women play knucklebones, versions of which are still played today. The tokens, called tali, *were made of animal bones, ivory, or other materials.*

Venus Throw, seems to have been one in which each die showed a different value. The worst throw was the Dog Throw, but its nature is not known. Players used a cup to prevent manipulation of the dice when throwing. [49]

In addition, gamblers used six-sided dice (*tesserae*) practically identical to modern ones.

Hunting and Mountain Climbing

More strenuous than playing board games and gambling, which required little physical effort, were two other leisure pastimes—hunting and climbing mountains. A few Romans, primarily poorer rural folk, hunted small game to help feed their families. But as a sport, hunting was most often a province of the upper classes, whose members could afford horses, hunting dogs, and gangs of slaves to carry supplies and dead game. It was not unusual, for instance, for well-to-do individuals to invite friends or business associates to their country estates to engage in hunting parties lasting several days.

These hunts rarely demanded much skill or courage from the participants, however,

This modern drawing of Roman hunters killing a wild boar is based on a scene from a wall painting found in an ancient tomb near Rome.

as there was often no actual pursuit involved. Instead, the hunters camped out in an area that animals frequented while their servants set up nets and traps. When the prey appeared, the servants and dogs drove the animals into the nets. Once the animals were caught and helpless, the hunters slew them with clubs, spears, or arrows. In a letter to the historian Tacitus, Pliny the Younger admits to spending most of his time on a recent hunt engaged in quiet study:

> I know you will think it a good joke, as indeed it is, when I tell you that your old friend [i.e., Pliny] has caught three boars, very fine ones, too. Yes, I really did, and without even changing any of my lazy holiday habits. I was sitting by the hunting nets with writing materials by my side instead of hunting spears. . . . So the next time you hunt yourself, follow my example and take your notebooks along with your lunch-basket and [wine] flask.[50]

In comparison to such mildly strenuous outings, mountain climbing required both good physical conditioning and a considerable expenditure of energy. For this reason, very few Romans braved steep, rugged hillsides except when their profession compelled them to, as in the cases of herdsmen, soldiers, and traders. Still, evidence has survived indicating that a few people climbed mountains for either the physical challenge or the rewarding panoramas visible from the summits. According to the first-century B.C. Greek traveler Strabo, Sicily's volcanic peak,

Mount Etna (which is still active today), was a favorite of Roman climbers. He says that it had lookouts at strategic locations, huts with sleeping facilities, and other amenities installed for the benefit of climbers. "Near the town of Centoripa is a small village called Etna," he writes in his noted treatise *Geography,*

> which takes in climbers and sends them on their way, for the ridge of the mountain begins here. Those who had recently climbed the summit told me that at the top was a level plain. . . . Two of their party were courageous enough to venture into the plain of the crater, but since the sand on which they were walking was becoming hotter and deeper, they turned back. [51]

Swimming and Boating

For the average Roman, however, taking a refreshing dip in a swimming pool was far preferable to risking life and limb on the slopes of an active volcano. Many bath-houses were equipped with pools. And most wealthy people, including Pliny the Younger, had either indoor or outdoor pools, or both. "There is a [heated] pool in the courtyard," Pliny writes in a letter describing his Tuscan villa, "and a well near it to tone you up with

A Dangerous Boat Race

This is part of the exciting boat race that appears in Virgil's epic poem the Aeneid *(Patric Dickinson's translation). It effectively captures the potential dangers involved in such contests.*

[The rowers] made a supreme effort; the brazen keel shuddered under the pulse of their mighty strokes. The sea slipped under them. Their throats were parched, their lungs were almost bursting, their sweat poured off in streams. And a sheer chance brought to the heroes the honor they coveted; for Sergestus [one of the captains], in a fever of excitement, kept bearing in towards the rocks and thrusting on the inside berth [racing lane], with lessening room to maneuver, until he ran, by ill luck, onto a reef. The very rock shuddered; against the jagged edges of flint the oars splintered and broke; the prow hung high and dry. . . . Mnestheus [another captain] now was jubilant and madder than ever to win, and with the wind at his beck and call and his oarsmen striking a fast rate, he scudded over the open water landward. . . . In the *Pristis* now Mnestheus skimmed through the last lanes of water as the wake of the boat simply propelled her onward. Sergestus he left behind, still in the toils of the reef and shallows, calling in vain for help.

cold water when you have had enough of the warm." [52]

Many Romans also swam in rivers, lakes, and the sea. Cicero, Ovid, and Horace all describe swimming in the Tiber River. The coasts of Italy, Greece, and Spain had many lovely beaches that regularly drew swimmers and sunbathers. And Pliny the Younger writes about the attractive beaches surrounding "a navigable lagoon" near Hippo, a town on the Mediterranean coast of North Africa. "People of all ages spend their time here," he says,

> to enjoy the pleasures of fishing, boating, and swimming, especially the boys, who have plenty of time to play. It is a bold feat with them to swim out into deep water, the winner being the one who has left the shore and his fellow-swimmers farthest behind. [53]

Pliny's mention of boating along with swimming in this passage touches on the fact that some Romans, especially those who lived in coastal regions, enjoyed sailing and rowing as leisure pastimes. Many well-to-do people had their own boats, but rentals were widely available for boating enthusiasts of ordinary means. A few of these individuals likely entered boat races, though little evidence survives for where and how often such events were held. Virgil includes an exciting depiction of ships racing in his *Aeneid*. Though fictional, it probably captures some elements of such races in his own time.

Athletics and Boxing

While the Romans enjoyed sporting activities such as ball playing, hunting, swimming, and boating as leisure fun, they were not very enthusiastic about the athletic competitions, including the renowned Olympic Games, that had long been popular among the Greeks. These contests included track-and-field events such as footraces, the broad jump, and the discus and javelin throws, as well as wrestling, probably the most widely practiced Greek sport. In fact, most Romans drew a clear line between these activities and the more violent public games, especially fights to the death between gladiators and bloody arena "hunts" in which armed men slaughtered captured animals. The only Greek Olympic-style sports that the Romans eagerly adopted were boxing and chariot racing; however, the Roman versions were almost always more violent and bloody than the Greek ones.

Regarding the question of why most Romans lacked interest in traditional Greek athletics, part of the answer lay in the Greek custom of competing in the nude. The average Roman viewed this practice as unmanly and even immoral. Another reason revolved around the issue of citizen participation in sporting events. Greek tradition encouraged and glorified such participation. In contrast, although most Romans thoroughly enjoyed watching large-scale violent games, which they saw as entertainment, for a Roman citizen actually to take part in such public spectacles was seen as undignified and socially unacceptable. This was largely a matter of honor. The Romans were extremely proud of their military skills and conquests and felt there was no greater disgrace than losing in battle.

Defeat in a sports contest was simply too much like defeat in war.

Over time, however, continued close contact with Greek culture caused the Roman dislike of Greek games to soften somewhat. In the late first century B.C., Augustus established a Greek-style athletic competition, the Actian Games, to celebrate his greatest military victory—the defeat of his rivals Antony and Cleopatra at Actium (in western Greece). Some eight decades later, the emperor Nero held similar games in Rome. During these years, some Roman citizens began attending such events along with Greeks. Yet these Romans were not representative of most of their countrymen, who still looked down on, or at least ignored, such contests.

The main exception was the combat sport of boxing, which many Romans came to love almost as much as gladiatorial bouts. Ancient boxing, both Greek and Roman versions, was significantly more strenuous and dangerous than its modern counterpart. There were many serious injuries, particularly to the face and head. And those boxers who remained conscious and refused to surrender were sometimes beaten to death. Today, boxers spar in a series of rounds, with rest periods in between; when a fighter goes down, his opponent must wait until he gets up before hitting him again. In ancient boxing, by contrast, there were no rounds or rest periods and hitting an opponent when he was down was permitted.

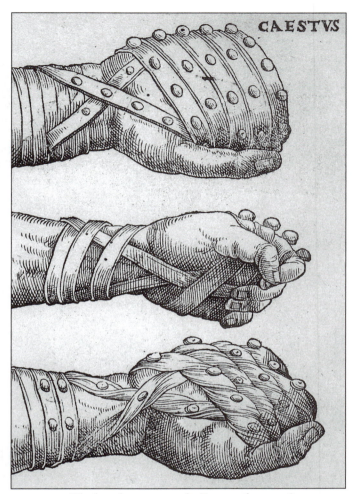

The hand gear worn by Roman boxers often caused serious injuries.

Most of the actual physical damage in such bouts was caused by the hand gear (today called gloves) worn by ancient boxers. By the early Empire, Greek boxers wore hardened leather pads around their knuckles, creating a fairly sharp edge that could easily cut into an opponent's flesh. The hand gear worn by Roman boxers was even more dangerous. Called a *caestus,* it was similar to

Roman boxers spar in this engraving. The sport was extremely dangerous, often causing permanent injury or death, yet the public loved it.

the Greek version except that it sometimes continued up the arm almost to the shoulder. Also, the knuckle area of the *caestus* featured a cluster of metal lumps and spikes, some of them two or three inches long. Not surprisingly, such gear could inflict appalling, even lethal damage. In the *Aeneid,* Virgil describes a boxer whose *caestus* is covered with bloodstains and pieces of human brain. Such matches were quite obviously far from relaxing for the participants, yet for Roman spectators they constituted one of the more popular and enduring of the many leisure pursuits they enjoyed.

Blood in the Sand: The Gladiators

The Romans loved large-scale entertainments, especially the kinds that involved danger and the potential for bloodshed and death. And gladiatorial combats were near the top of their list of most popular leisure pastimes. During the twentieth century much was written about why the Romans not only saw nothing wrong with watching people kill one another but also enjoyed it. A number of early modern scholars assumed that they must have been a cruel and bloodthirsty people, but that view is now antiquated.

Instead, it appears that the Roman fascination for gladiators and death in the arena was part of a worldview and a value system considerably different than those accepted in modern Western society. "In

our own age," scholar Alan Baker points out,

> human life is prized and respected above all else (at least in theory); to inflict suffering on others for the sake of enjoyment is considered perverse and incomprehensible. But such a perspective simply did not exist in the ancient world. [54]

Among the ancients, especially the Romans, military culture and values, including naked conquest, were widely accepted and glorified, and these martial values were reflected in other aspects of society, including entertainment.

Also, the combat and death of a gladiator was seen as conforming to deeply held

A Bad Reputation

The Romans had strong and highly contradictory feelings about gladiators. When these warriors were fighting and dying in the arena, crowds saw them as heroes and men of honor and cheered them. But outside the arena, gladiators were widely viewed as nearly worthless social inferiors. The bad reputations of gladiators and other arena fighters negatively affected their public image, self-esteem, social opportunities, and much more. Common words used to describe them included crude, indecent, hopeless, and damned. Also, writers, most of whom were upper class, regularly ridiculed them and compared them to socially unacceptable characters like prostitutes, criminals, and effeminate actors. Part of this attitude stemmed from the fact that most gladiators started out as slaves or prisoners; however, even those who earned their freedom (or were free when they became gladiators) were treated no better than slaves. Gladiators could not escape their bad reputations even by dying. They were not allowed to be buried in public cemeteries, and only when a relative, friend, or kindhearted fan claimed the body and buried it privately could a gladiator be assured of a proper funeral.

beliefs about the nature of honor and the virtue of submission to higher authority. To a Roman, such submission, whether to a patron, the emperor, or the gods, was part of the natural order, something expected of everyone. And when gladiators fought, they submitted themselves to the will and mercy of their audience. This made them, at least for that moment, heroic figures, models for persons of honor and integrity not unlike soldiers who fought and died for the fatherland.

The Roman fascination for and moral acceptance of gladiatorial fights, called *munera* (singular, *munos*), was also rooted in ancient tradition. In Rome's early cen-

turies, combat to the death between two warriors was a part of funeral ritual in some Italian regions, especially Campania (a fertile region about two hundred miles south of Rome). The belief was that when a prominent man died it was necessary to supply his spirit with a sacrifice of human blood. At first, this was accomplished by killing a war captive near the tomb; over time, the custom changed to having two prisoners fight each other at the grave site.

As the centuries elapsed, these ceremonies grew more elaborate and began to draw increasing numbers of spectators. And because they were exciting and compelling, people came to see them more as entertainment than as funeral ritual. By the last years of the Republic, the *munera* had become major attractions at large-scale public games, events eagerly attended by Romans of all walks of life.

Settings for Death

To reconstruct what a typical *munus* was like for these thrill seekers, one must first consider the setting. The combats took place in large oval-shaped structures known as amphitheaters (*amphitheatri*). At first, they were temporary and made of wood, as in the case of theaters, but as the gladiatorial bouts gained in popularity, people saw the need for permanent stone versions. Italy's first stone amphitheater was constructed in Pompeii (in Campania) in about 80 B.C. The

Pairs of fighters grapple at an early funeral in Rome. Eventually, this custom evolved into combats between professional gladiators in public games.

structure is beautifully preserved thanks to the A.D. 79 eruption of nearby Mount Vesuvius, which encased it in a protective layer of ash. The building measured 445 by 341 feet and sat about twenty thousand people in its heyday.

In the years that followed, other amphitheaters sprang up across the Roman world. The largest and most impressive of all—the Colosseum in Rome—opened the year after Vesuvius's eruption. The Colosseum measured 620 by 513 feet in breadth and over 156 feet in height. The oval arena floor, where the gladiators fought, was 287 feet long by 180 feet wide. And the seating capacity was in the neighborhood of fifty thousand.

When they entered the Colosseum to witness a *munus*, the spectators first searched for suitable seats. The place one sat depended on his or her status. The emperor,

This twentieth-century watercolor reconstructs what the Colosseum looked like in its glory days, when gladiatorial bouts and wild beast shows were held there.

senators, and other dignitaries sat in a low section, just above the arena, where they had an excellent view of the action. Ordinary citizens sat higher and farther away, and women and slaves were confined to the bleachers near the top.

Whatever their seating arrangements, all spectators enjoyed various comforts and amenities. Among these were statues, tapestries, and other ornate decorations; cushions to sit on; cookshops surrounding the complex and vendors selling refreshments in the stands; and a huge awning (*velarium*) that shaded the audience on hot, sunny days. The awning was a must because the Mediterranean sun can be very intense and easily cause sunburn or heatstroke.

A Colorful Array of Fighters

By the time that most of the spectators had seated themselves, the festivities began. First came the *pompa,* a colorful and stately parade in which the gladiators strode into the arena accompanied by acrobats, jugglers, and musicians playing marching music. Eventually all but the fighters exited. The musicians moved to a safe position and prepared to play "background" music during the matches. Then, supervised by the official who ran the event, the gladiators drew lots to determine who would fight whom. Next, the official— or on occasion the emperor himself—inspected the fighters' weapons to ensure they were well sharpened. And finally, the gladiators raised their weapons toward the emperor or highest-ranking official present and shouted, *"Morituri te salutant!"* ("Those about to die salute you!")

During all these preliminaries, the spectators had a chance to get a good look at the fighters and see which types would be sparring that day. Modern scholars are unsure about how many different kinds of gladiators existed by the early Roman Empire. There were at least six or seven distinct types, and there may have been as many as twenty or more. The earliest and major gladiator type was the Samnite, named after, outfitted, and armed like the Samnite warriors (of central Italy) who fought and suffered defeat by Rome in the fourth century B.C. "The Samnite was a heavily armed man," writes Eckart Kohne, an authority on gladiators, "with a helmet (probably of the kind with a brim and crest), a large [rectangular] shield (*scutum*), a sword, and probably a greave [lower-leg protector] on the left leg." [55] The Samnite also wore an arm guard (*manica*) on his sword arm.

The audiences at the Colosseum never saw a classic Samnite fighter because this type had disappeared by the early Empire. However, they enjoyed the fighting skills of several gladiator types that were slight variations on the Samnite. One was the *hoplomachus.* He looked similar to a Samnite, except that he carried a round rather than rectangular shield and wielded a spear as well as a sword. Another Samnite-like gladiator, the *secutor,* had the rectangular shield, but his helmet was more rounded and protective, with tiny eyeholes. Kohne describes the *myrmillo,* another descendant of the Samnite, this way:

The *myrmillo* fought with his torso bare. He wore the *manica* on his right

Much of what is known about the armor and weapons of various kinds of gladiators comes from surviving mosaics. This one was found at Lepcis Magna, in North Africa.

arm . . . [and a brimmed helmet] on which a plume of feathers or more frequently horsehair could be placed. . . . The shield (*scutum*) was a tall oblong, curved like the section of a cylinder. . . . The *myrmillo* had only one weapon of attack, a short to medium-length sword with a broad, straight blade, a *gladius* [the same weapon carried by Roman soldiers].[56]

Other gladiator types that were favorites with crowds included the Thracian (or Thrax), who fought with a short curved sword (*sica*) and small round shield; and the *retiarius*, or "net man," who wore no helmet, little armor, and wielded a net and tri-

dent (three-pronged spear). Among the less common types was the *dimachaerius*. He carried no shield and fought with two swords (or daggers), one held in each hand. Another kind of gladiator, the *laquearius*, used a lasso to entangle, immobilize, and choke his opponent, whereas *equites* fought on horseback and *essedarii* on chariots. Probably the oddest of the lot was the *andabate*, who fought wearing a helmet with no eyeholes. *Andabates* were paired only against one another, as it would have been grossly unfair to pit a blindfolded person against one who could see. There were female gladiators, too. Far less common than her male brethren, the gladiatrix was banned from Roman arenas in the early second century.

Win, Lose, or Draw

When it was time for the fighters representing the various gladiator types to commence combat, all exited the Colosseum except for the two scheduled for the first match. As they began to take each other's measure and finally their weapons clashed, the spectators reacted loudly, some cheering for one fighter, others for his or her opponent. There was usually no telling who would win, but the audience members were well aware of the many possible outcomes for any given match. The most common of these can be seen in the lists compiled at the end of each *munus,* some of which have survived. Each list gives the names of the fighters, along with a capital letter. A P stood for *periit,* meaning "perished," a V for *vicit,* meaning "won," and an M for *missus,* meaning a loser whose life was spared.

All of these outcomes involved a clear winner and loser. But a draw might result in a match in which both warriors fought well and could not defeat each other. Each of the fighters in such a bout was said to be *stans missus* ("allowed to leave"). This shows that "there was an underlying principle of justice" in the *munera,* Baker suggests.

The Gladiatrix

Women gladiators became fashionable from time to time. (Usually they fought one another or male dwarves.) The emperor Domitian (reigned A.D. 81–96) was particularly fond of them and featured them often, for example. However, the gladiatrix bore even more of a social stigma than male gladiators, as shown in this biting excerpt from one of Juvenal's satires (Peter Green's translation).

We've all seen *them* [the female gladiators during training], stabbing the stump with a foil [sword], shield well advanced, going through the proper motions. . . . The goal of all their practice is the real arena. But then, what modesty can be looked for in some helmeted vixen, a renegade from her sex, who thrives on masculine violence—yet would not prefer to *be* a man, since the pleasure is so much less? What a fine sight for some husband—*it might be you*—his wife's equipment put up at auction, sword-belt, armlet, plumes [helmet decorations], and one odd shin-guard! Or, if the other style of fighting takes her fancy, imagine your delight when the dear girl sells off her greaves! . . . Note how she snorts at each practice thrust, bowed down by the weight of her helmet . . . then wait for the laugh, when she lays down her weapons and squats over the potty!

The audience expected to be entertained by a good, professional performance, and if a gladiator fought bravely and well, he could reasonably expect to be allowed to leave the arena alive, even if his opponent defeated him. From the Roman point of view, fighting bravely and dying nobly were of enormous moral importance, and any gladiator who found favor with his audience in these terms could frequently count on their willingness to allow him to leave the arena. [57]

Numerous ancient inscriptions mention this outcome, so it was likely fairly common. Noted classical historian Michael Grant cites the case of one fighter for whom evidence has survived: "The epitaph of the gladiator Flamma, who lived to the age of thirty, records that he won twenty-five contests, with *missus* four times, and *stans missus* nine times." [58] In stark contrast to such draws was a completely uncompromising situation— the *sine missione,* in which the combatants were ordered to continue fighting until one slew the other. Overall, the evidence suggests that the *sine missione* was not as common as the *stans missus.*

Gladiatorial bouts unfolded in other ways as well. Sometimes the fighters were physically unimpressive or neither combatant put his heart into his work, which disappointed or even angered the onlookers.

Roman spectators watch a fight between a retiarius *and a* myrmillo. *The man on the horse is a referee, who had the authority to stop or discipline the combatants.*

A defeated gladiator gestures for mercy from the crowd in French artist Jean Gerome's oil painting, Pollice Verso *("Thumbs Down").*

The punishment for such a poor display could be a beating or whipping. "What good has Norbanus done us?" a character in the *Satyricon* asks about a wealthy man who had sponsored a *munus*.

> He put on some half-pint gladiators, so done-in already that they'd have dropped if you blew on them. I've seen animal killers [most of whom had less training than gladiators] fight better. . . . One boy did have a little spirit— he was in Thracian armor and even he didn't show any initiative. In fact, they were all flogged afterwards [for failing to fight well], there were so many shouts of "Give 'em what for!" from the crowd. Pure yellow [cowardice], that's all. [59]

Deciding a Gladiator's Fate

Surely one of the more common occurrences witnessed by the crowds at the Colosseum was when one fighter wounded the other, causing him or her to fall to the ground. Following custom, the downed gladiator then raised one finger, signaling a plea for mercy. The rules, which were strictly observed, forbade this person from making another move, particularly any attempt to carry on the fight. All he or she could do was lay there quietly and submit to the will of the highest-ranking official present, who often went along with the spectators' wishes in deciding the gladiator's fate.

These "judges" in the crowd signaled their desire through hand gestures. The traditional view, that a "thumbs-up" meant life and a "thumbs-down" death, is still plausible, but may well be incorrect. A number of scholars now contend that a "thumbs-down," reinforced by waving handkerchiefs, was the signal for the winner to drop his sword and spare the loser, while the signal for death was turning the thumb inward toward the chest, symbolizing a sword jabbed into the heart. Another theory suggests that a spectator called for death by pointing a thumb toward his or her throat since the victor usually executed his opponent by a sword thrust to the throat.

Though it might seem possible for a fallen fighter to escape this gruesome fate by playing dead, it is likely that no one ever got away with such a ruse. The arena rituals in which the bodies were cleared away included safeguards to expose fakers, as Baker explains:

> Upon the death of a gladiator, an attendant dressed as Charon [in mythology the boatman who ferried dead souls across the river bordering the Underworld] . . . entered the arena and struck the prone fighter with a mallet. . . . He was followed by another attendant, dressed as [the god] Mercury, who traditionally escorted the souls of the dead to the Underworld. "Mercury" carried a wand . . . which was really a red-hot branding iron, with which he would prod the body of the fallen gladiator. . . . The dead man was then carried away on a stretcher, or sometimes a long hook would be sunk into his flesh and his corpse dragged away by a horse. [60]

State Executions and Impromptu Gladiators

The gladiators who took part in these bloody displays did not confine their lethal attacks only to one another. The spectators at the Colosseum and other amphitheaters often witnessed another form of killing—arena executions. By order of the state, gladiators frequently slaughtered convicted criminals. These unfortunate individuals had been found guilty of various offenses and had been assigned the dreadful designation of *noxii ad gladium ludi damnati,* meaning "condemned to be killed by the sword in the games." The official in charge of the *munera* kept the condemned in detention cells and promised to execute each no more than a year after he or she had been sentenced.

These executions usually took place around noon, a grisly interlude between the wild beast hunts that occurred in the amphitheater in the morning and the formal gladiatorial combats staged in the afternoon. In one style of execution, guards removed the unarmed criminals from their cells and led them into the arena. There, it was common for some jesters to mock the condemned as well as pretend to kill one another in a macabre display of comic relief before the actual commencement of bloodletting. Perhaps this went on until the spectators grew restless, a signal that they were bored and desired for the "show" to go on. Finally, a group of fully armed gladiators appeased them by attacking and killing the prisoners.

However, a number of other modes of execution were common, including one in which two condemned prisoners fought each other, making them in a sense impromptu amateur gladiators. When their match ended, another pair was herded onto the blood-soaked sands and so forth until all of the prisoners were dead. "The first two stood facing each other in the arena," one scholar effectively describes it.

Neither of them had any gladiatorial training, neither wore any armor, and only one held a dagger. It was thus virtually certain that the armed man would kill his opponent. Both men understood this, and so the unarmed man decided . . . that the only thing to do was to run from his opponent as fast as he could. . . . Almost at once, a large group of servants appeared, carrying whips and glowing branding irons. They closed in on the fleeing man and went to work on him, the sound of cracking whips and the smoke rising from the burning flesh placating the crowd. [Eventually] the unarmed man . . . was driven towards his waiting opponent. The battle was short-lived. The dagger-wielder lunged and planted his weapon in the center of the other's chest. He dropped without a sound, and was hauled away. . . . Another condemned criminal then entered the arena. The first was forced to surrender his weapon to him, and became the defenseless

"Murder Pure and Simple"

At least a few Romans viewed the arena executions as distasteful and not a constructive use of a decent person's time. One who felt this way was the philosopher and playwright Seneca, who penned this tract (quoted in Robin Campbell's collection of Seneca's letters) after witnessing the execution of a group of unarmed condemned men.

I happened to go to one of these shows at the time of the lunch-hour interlude, expecting there to be some light and witty entertainment then, some respite for the purpose of affording people's eyes a rest from human blood. Far from it. All the earlier contests were charity in comparison. The nonsense is dispensed with now. What we have now is murder pure and simple. The combatants have nothing to protect them; their whole bodies are exposed to the blows. Every thrust they launch gets home. A great many spectators prefer this to the ordinary matches. . . . And quite naturally. There are no helmets and no shields repelling the weapons. What is the point of armor? Or of skill? All that sort of thing just makes the death slower in coming.

quarry. It was not long before he, too, lay on the sand, his neck open and pumping out blood. [61]

Still other forms of arena execution included crucifixion and tying the condemned to stakes to be eaten by half-starved lions, panthers, bears, and other beasts. Whether gladiators, animals, or the prisoners themselves did the actual killing, custom dictated that it was offensive to dead and departed emperors to have to "witness" the execution of common criminals. So attendants used pieces of fabric to veil any emperors' statues or busts erected in the am-phitheater. According to ancient sources, the emperor Claudius held so many executions that he ordered the removal of a statue of Augustus rather than allow it to be almost perpetually veiled.

Meanwhile, the ordinary spectators waited for the executions to end and the full-fledged gladiatorial bouts to begin. For them, one-on-one battles between trained warriors was the ultimate duel to the death, whereas the executions were merely an interesting diversion. In the Colosseum and in other Roman amphitheaters, gladiators were always the main attraction.

Chapter

7

Arena Hunters
and Their Prey

The audiences who crowded the Colosseum and other amphitheaters to see gladiators fight to the death also enjoyed a wide variety of animal shows. Including fights between beasts and humans, battles between beasts and beasts, trained animals acts, and the execution of criminals by beasts, they bore the collective name of *venationes* (singular, *venatio*). This Latin term translates as "hunts." It is unfortunately not very descriptive of these shows. The animal acts and executions had nothing to do with hunting, and even the fights did not qualify as hunting in the classic sense—that is, sportsmen stalking wild creatures in their natural habitats.

At any rate, the *venationes* began as small-scale warm-ups for the *munera* and over time grew into popular attractions in their own right. In the words of Roland Auguet, an authority on Rome's public games:

> The *venatio* was a sort of substantial hors d'oeuvre [appetizer]; as clearly defined spectacle, it came into being later than the gladiatorial combats, with which it was almost always associated. It was customary for a *munus* to be accompanied by a hunt, the object of which . . . was to enhance its brilliance. From the end of the Republic, however, the *venationes* took on such proportions as, in certain exceptional cases, to constitute a spectacle in its own right attended for its own sake; they

87

then took place in the late afternoon and no longer in the slack morning hours. Some, moreover, as the inscriptions testify, lasted for several days. [62]

It is not surprising that so many Romans enjoyed spending some of their leisure hours watching the beast shows. Animals, especially exotic ones, had been popular in Rome long before the public hunts began to be presented in amphitheaters. The Roman fondness for animals can perhaps be attributed to their being a pastoral people. On their farms and country estates, they raised donkeys, horses, cattle, pigs, and other domesticated animals. And eventually, as Rome conquered other parts of the known world, military generals began displaying creatures from distant lands in their victory parades in the capital.

In this way the Roman populace was introduced to elephants (which they called "Lucanian cows") in the early third century B.C. About a century later ostriches ("sea sparrows"), leopards ("African mice"), and lions were first seen in Italy. The first hippopotamus and crocodile came in 58 B.C., the first rhinoceros in 55 B.C., and the first giraffe in 46 B.C. Although some of these animals (including monkeys and even lions and

A modern reconstruction of arena hunters fighting animals in the amphitheater at Pompeii. Over the centuries, millions of animals were slaughtered this way.

An Italian engraving shows Roman hunters capturing lions for the arena. Tigers, panthers, bulls, ostriches, and especially elephants were also in high demand.

elephants) were made into pets, most became attractions in the *venationes*.

Acquiring the Animals: A Costly Process

Several thousand new animals were required for these shows each year in the Colosseum alone. So the number needed for all of the Roman amphitheaters each year must have been in the tens of thousands. The process of catching them and transporting them to Rome and other cities was complicated, costly, and required the services of hundreds and at times thousands of people of diverse backgrounds and skills.

Among these specialists were skilled hunters who stalked and ensnared beasts in all sections of the Roman world and in lands lying far beyond it. For example, elephants derived from northern and central Africa or

on occasion from faraway India; tigers from India and northern Persia; lions and leopards from Africa and Syria; bears from Africa, central Europe, and Italy itself; horses from Spain; exotic species of dogs from Britain; and crocodiles from Egypt. Usually the hunters used leg traps, nets, or deep pits to capture their prey. Pits were often used to ensnare elephants, for instance, as described here by Pliny the Elder. He begins by noting that this animal's high degree of intelligence presented a challenge to the hunters:

> An elephant that accidentally encounters a man wandering across its path in some remote place is mild and quiet and even, it is said, points out the way. Yet the very same animal, when it notices a man's footprint, trembles in fear of an ambush before catching sight of

Lions on the Loose

In this excerpt from his Life of Brutus (*in* Makers of Rome) *Plutarch recounts the incident in which lions bound for the amphitheater were let loose in the Greek city of Megara.*

These animals had been left at Megara, and when the city was captured by Calenus [one of Julius Caesar's officers, who had been ordered to pacify southern Greece during the civil war then raging], Caesar appropriated them for himself. They are said to have brought disaster to Megara, because when the city was on the point of being captured, the Megarians broke open the cages and unchained them, hoping that they would attack the enemy as they entered the city. But, instead of this, the lions turned against the unarmed Megarians and tore them to pieces as they ran to and fro in terror, so that even their enemies were overcome with pity at the sight.

the man himself; he [the elephant] stops to pick up the scent, looks about him, and trumpets in anger . . . and passes [a warning] to the next elephant, and that one to the one following. . . . In India, they are rounded up by a mahout [elephant driver], who, riding a tame elephant, either catches a wild one on its own, or separates one from the herd and beats it so that when it is exhausted he can mount it and control it in the same way as the tame one. Africans employ covered pits to trap elephants. When one strays into a pit, the rest of the herd immediately heap branches together, roll down rocks, and . . . [use] every effort to drag it out.[63]

After capturing elephants and other beasts for the games, the hunters delivered them to individuals who specialized in transporting the creatures to the cities. Having reached a city, the animals were at first kept in a holding area, which had cages specially designed for the task; only when the official in charge of the games signaled that he was ready did the handlers bring the creatures to the amphitheater. While in such holding areas, the animals had to be well fed and also closely watched to make sure they did not get loose. In one unfortunate incident, a leopard escaped its cage on a dock near Rome and killed a sculptor who was attempting to make a clay model of a caged lion. Another fatal incident occurred in the Greek city of Megara in 48 B.C. Some of the residents opened cages containing lions, hoping the big cats would attack Julius Caesar's soldiers who were threatening the city. But the lions turned on the Megarians instead.

The Arena Hunters

When the captured animals finally made it to an amphitheater like the Colosseum, they were kept in cages in a maze of chambers and corridors located directly beneath the arena floor. Their fate was sealed because soon they would have to fight either one another or an arena hunter to the death. Such a hunter was called a *venator.* Another term for a hunter was *bestiarius,* meaning "beast man." The two labels may have been more or less interchangeable; however, many scholars believe that the term *bestiarii* was applied to lower-status hunters or hunters who fought in a style markedly different from that of the *venatores.* (The *venatores* trained in a special school similar to the kind attended by gladiators, although the hunters likely received less comprehensive and rigorous training than gladiators did.)

For a weapon, a *venator* most often used a *venabulum,* a spear with an iron head. He could either throw it at an animal, like a whaler harpooning his prey, or hold the spear outward and try to impale a charging beast on it. If he missed in either case, he could be in serious trouble. "Clothed for the most part in a simple, close-fitting tunic," Auguet points out, the hunters "had no protection other than leather bands on the arms and legs; the weapon in their hands thus became their only hope of salvation." [64]

The hunters used other weapons as well, including bows and arrows, swords, clubs, and daggers. Some fighters used only the bow, while others specialized in attacking a single species of animal. Those who fought bulls, the *taurarii,* resembled modern-day matadors. Sometimes they tried to stab lances into the creatures; other times, a *taurarius* jumped from horseback onto a bull, seized it by the horns, and tried to wrestle it to the ground, as seen in modern rodeos.

Such displays were certain to please the fans cheering loudly in the stands. And the more successful *venatores* became popular heroes almost on a par with winning charioteers and gladiators. Martial penned this glowing tribute to one of the most successful of all the Roman arena hunters, Carpophorus, who fought in the Colosseum in the A.D. 80s:

> He plunged his spear in a charging bear, once prime in the peak of the

A detail from a mosaic depicts a venator *spearing a charging leopard.*

Arctic pole [possibly a reference to a polar bear]; he laid low a lion of unprecedented size, a sight to see, who might have done honor to Hercules' hands [a reference to the mythical character who was credited with slaying the powerful Nemean lion]; he stretched dead a fleet leopard with a wound felt from afar. [65]

Even as such hunters made their kills, beasts were forced to fight their fellow beasts. The animals were raised from the holding area below and onto the arena floor via hand-operated elevators, and they jumped into the spectators' view through trapdoors. Sometimes two creatures would attack each other, but other times they had to be coaxed. One common method was to chain the two together so that sooner or later, as they tried to free themselves, they would become anxious, angry, and begin fighting. Seneca describes such a battle between a bull and a panther that were tethered together. Eventually, if one (or both) of the mangled animals was still alive, armed "executioners" (*confectores*) moved in and finished it off.

Objections to the Hunts

Such pitiless slaughter of nearly helpless animals strikes most people today as cruel. Why, then, did the Romans see the arena hunts as entertainment? First, like a number of other ancient peoples, they were fascinated by the phenomenon of death and were certain that it held some mystical connection to life. In some of his epigrams, Martial explores this notion, reflecting a common belief of

his day that the gods or fate played an instrumental role in the lives and deaths of people and animals. As an example, he cites an incident in a *venatio* in which a baby pig sprang from its mother's womb only seconds after a hunter killed her. "Amid the cruel perils of Caesar's hunt," he begins,

a light spear had pierced a pregnant sow. One of her litter leapt out of the hapless mother's wound. Savage Lucina [a side of the personality of the goddess of the hunt, Diana, believed by many to assist in childbirth], was *this* a delivery? She would have wished to die wounded by further weapons, so that the sad path [from the womb] might open for all her brood. Who denies that [the god] Bacchus sprang from his mother's death? Believe that a deity was so given birth; so born was a beast. [66]

Another reason that many Romans enjoyed watching the *venationes* was that it became a cultural tradition. Parents in each succeeding generation brought up their children to think that this aspect of the public games was a normal leisure pursuit.

On the other hand, not every Roman viewed it as either fair or ethical for humans to slaughter animals (or for animals to kill people) in this manner. As revealed in their writings, a number of intellectuals, including Cicero, viewed the arena hunts as pointless and disturbing. He recorded his feelings in a letter to a like-minded friend after attending a *venatio* sponsored by the noted military general Pompey in 55 B.C.:

Dwindling Supplies of Animals

Because so many animals were captured for the arena hunts over the course of centuries, their populations naturally shrank in some areas, making it difficult to find samples of some species. Cicero alludes to this problem in a letter written when he was governor of the province of Cilicia (in southern Asia Minor). In the summer of 51 B.C. his friend Marcus Caelius Rufus took charge of staging animals shows in Rome and begged Cicero to send him some Cilician panthers for his upcoming games. This excerpt from an exchange between the two men is from Jo-Ann Shelton's translation in her As the Romans Did.

Caelius to Cicero: In almost all my letters to you I have written about the panthers. . . . If you but remember, and if you send for some hunters . . . then you will satisfy my request. I am greatly concerned about this now. . . . So please, dear friend, take on this task. . . . As soon as the panthers have been caught, you have with you the men I sent over on financial business to feed them and arrange for shipping.

Cicero to Caelius: About the panthers! The matter is being handled with diligence and according to my orders by men who are skillful hunters. But there is a remarkable scarcity of panthers. And they tell me that the few panthers left are complaining bitterly that they are the only animals in my province for whom traps are set. And therefore they have decided, or so the rumor goes, to leave my province and move to Caria [a nearby region of Asia Minor].

If it was some physical ailment or ill health which kept you from attending the spectacles, I would attribute your absence more to your luck than to your wisdom. . . . Things that won the applause of the common people would have given you no enjoyment. . . . There were wild animal hunts, two a day for five-days, very expensive ones—no one can deny that. But what pleasure can a civilized man find when either a helpless human being is mangled by a very strong animal, or a magnificent animal is stabbed again and again with a hunting spear? Even if this was something to look at, you have seen it often enough before, and I, who was a spectator there, saw nothing new. The last day was the day for elephants. The mob of spectators was greatly impressed, but showed no real enjoyment. In fact, a certain sympathy arose for the elephants, and a feeling that there was a kind of affinity between that large animal and the human race.[67]

The Issue of Security

Years later Pliny the Elder provided more detail about the treatment of the elephants in this same show. "One elephant put up a fantastic fight," he writes,

> and although its feet were badly wounded, [it] crawled on its knees against the attacking bands [of hunters]. It snatched away their shields and hurled them into the air. . . . There was also an extraordinary incident with a second elephant when it was killed by a single blow: a javelin struck under its eye and penetrated the vital parts of its head. All the elephants *en masse* [in a group], tried to break out through the iron railings that enclosed them, much to the discomfiture of the spectators. . . . But when Pompey's elephants had given up hope of escape, they played on the sympathy of the crowd, entreating them with indescribable gestures. They moaned, as if wailing, and caused the spectators such distress that, forgetting Pompey and his lavish display . . . they rose in a body, in tears, and heaped dire curses on Pompey, the effects of which he soon suffered. [68]

When the elephants in Pompey's show "tried to break out," many in the crowd were naturally frightened. Indeed, safety and security in the hunts was seen as an important issue by the fans and the games officials alike. The iron railings at Pompey's games only barely managed to keep the huge beasts from hurting the spectators. Probably with this and similar incidents in mind, when

Caesar presented a *venatio* a few years later (46 B.C.), he made sure to install stronger security measures. He ordered the digging of a moat ten feet wide and the same depth between the audience and arena floor.

Later, when the Colosseum was erected, it featured a thirteen-foot-high wall surrounding the arena. There was also a wooden barrier and a huge net to discourage frightened or desperate beasts from reaching the crowd. Such measures, adopted in all subsequent *venationes,* must have been effective since no evidence has survived indicating that any spectator was either injured or killed by an animal during a hunt.

Trained Animal Acts

The safety measures aside, the atmosphere of danger at the hunts was not constant. In between the bloodier events, and often following them, the spectators enjoyed a variety of amusing or charming acts performed by trained animals. Among the more popular were monkeys, who were often dressed as soldiers and drove miniature chariots drawn by goats. Dogs performed, too. Plutarch wrote that he saw one of these amazing canines pretend to eat poison, die, and then come back to life. Bears climbed poles, and seals answered to their names by barking or waving their flippers. Auguet cites other examples:

> Tigers let themselves be kissed by their tamers; lions caught hares in full flight and made a point of honor to seize them gently in their jaws without a scratch; bulls lay on their backs displaying their bellies as their masters rode

them in chariots at full speed. Nothing, however, equaled the . . . docile elephants; they knew how to imitate the combats of the gladiators, how to take their seats at a banquet without overturning the tables, and how, four at a time, to carry on a litter one of their number representing a woman after childbirth, to saying nothing of . . . [dancing] or walking the tightrope. [69]

The most moving description of one of these trained elephants comes from the pen of Pliny the Elder. This pachyderm, he says, which was "somewhat slow-witted in understanding orders," suffered beatings when it made mistakes in the arena. The poor creature "was discovered at night practicing what he had to do [in the next show]." [70]

Criminals Executed by Animals

Completely different in tone than the light-hearted animal acts was perhaps the most gruesome aspect of the arena hunts—public executions in which wild beasts mangled, killed, and sometimes partially ate condemned criminals. In the earliest *venationes*, this horrible punishment was reserved for foreign-born Roman soldiers who deserted the ranks. Later it was expanded to include slaves, former slaves, and Christians who had been convicted of serious crimes. These condemned individuals were called *bestiarii*, the same term that described the low-level arena hunters.

As a rule, the animals to be used in an upcoming execution either were starved

Condemned men attempt to fend off attacking lions in a Roman arena. Some scholars think that the term bestiarius *was sometimes used to describe such men.*

A Rhino's Fury

This epigram by Martial (from D.R. Shackleton Bailey's translation) recalls the fury of a rhinoceros that had to be provoked into fighting during an arena hunt.

While the trembling trainers were goading the rhinoceros and the great beast's anger was long agathering, men were giving up hope [that it would fight]. But at length the fury we earlier knew returned. For with his double horn he tossed a heavy bear as a bull tosses dummies. . . . He lifted two steers with his mobile neck [and] to him yielded the fierce buffalo and bison. A lion fleeing before him ran headlong upon the spears.

for several days beforehand or were specially trained to attack humans. They appeared from the trapdoors on the arena floor and attacked the prisoners, who had been tied to poles. A more elaborate version that occurred from time to time was a reenactment of the execution of an infamous Roman brigand and murderer of republican times named Laureolus. In the first century B.C. the poet Catullus wrote a mime that dramatized Laureolus's punishment, and starting around A.D. 30 actors were hired to impersonate him in repeat performances of the mime held in amphitheaters. Finally, about a half-century later, these staged dramas took a grisly turn as a condemned criminal switched places with the actor at the last moment and experienced a real execution. After being nailed to a cross, he was mauled and partially eaten by a half-starved bear. "Laureolus, hanging on no sham cross, gave his naked flesh to a Caledonian bear," Martial wrote in an epigram.

His lacerated limbs lived on, dripping gore, and in all his body, body there was none [i.e., his body had lost its normal shape]. Finally he met with the punishment he deserved; the guilty wretch had plunged a sword into his father's throat or his master's, or in his madness had robbed a temple of its secret gold, or laid a cruel torch to Rome. The criminal had outdone the misdeeds of ancient story; in him, what had been a play became an execution.[71]

Such graphic executions constituted only a small part of the highly varied programs that drew large crowds to the Roman amphitheaters. Only two other public entertainments could top them in sheer size, grandeur, and spectacle—the chariot races and staged naval battles.

Chariot Races and Mock Naval Battles

The largest and most spectacular of all Roman entertainments were the chariot races (*ludi circenses*) and staged naval battles (*naumachiae*). The races, easily the most popular of the public games, were held in circuses, long structures equipped with oval racetracks. The naval battles usually took place on natural or artificial lakes. These shows were so huge, complex, and expensive to produce that they were not daily or even weekly events. Chariot races, most often held to celebrate various religious festivals and military victories, took place on no more than seventy days, in total, each year during the late first century A.D. The *naumachiae* were much less frequent, occurring once every few years. So when the news spread that one of these special shows would be presented, people from all over the region eagerly looked forward to them.

The Great Circus

As a result, chariot races always drew enormous crowds. Early in the morning on the day of a racing show, large numbers of people jammed into their local circus. The largest and most renowned of these facilities was the Circus Maximus (often called the Great Circus) in Rome. Filling much of the valley between the Palatine and Aventine Hills, it was truly one of the wonders of the ancient world. It measured some 680 yards (over a third of a mile) long and 150 yards wide, and the dirt track on which the racers competed was about 635 by 85 yards, or roughly twelve times the size of the arena floor of

The Roman Circus at Jerusalem, in Palestine, as reconstructed for the spectacular 1959 film Ben-Hur. *The Circus Maximus in Rome was even larger.*

the Colosseum. Modern scholars think that the seating sections of the Circus Maximus accommodated about 150,000 people. Some ancient sources mention a figure of 250,000, but this probably included the many spectators who stood on the hillsides overlooking the track.

Dominating the view of the racing fans as they filed into the Great Circus and searched for seats was a long, narrow stone barrier running down the middle of the track. Called the *euripus* (or *spina*), it was covered with shrines, altars, statues, and other monuments. The charioteers raced around this barrier, each circuit constituting a lap. A typical race consisted of seven laps, a total distance of about three miles. By the mid–first century A.D., the Circus Maximus featured twenty-four races a day.

Once the stands of the enormous racetrack had filled, the fans watched an elaborate preliminary show, a *pompa* similar to the kind preceding a *munus*, only much larger. The parade began on the sacred temple-lined Capitoline Hill and moved through the city's streets until it reached the Great Circus. Scholar Richard C. Beacham provides this thumbnail description based on various ancient evidence:

The presiding official rode in a chariot. . . . Heading the retinue on horseback were sons of the Roman nobility, followed on foot by other citizens' sons destined to serve in the infantry. Both groups were organized into military formation, and this part of the display served . . . to impress visiting foreigners with Rome's might. Next came those who would participate in the games, first the [chariot] drivers. . . . Groups of armed dancers followed . . . and were accompanied by [musicians]. The dancers wore purple tunics, elaborately plumed bronze helmets, and carried swords and short spears. . . . The armed dancers were followed by a dancing chorus of men . . . costumed in goats' skins and high hairy manes. . . . The final section of the procession . . . consisted of embellished images of the gods, carried in chariots or on trays. [72]

The Charioteers

Upon entering the racetrack, the hundreds, and sometimes thousands, of people taking part in the *pompa* slowly wound their way around the *euripus* while the crowd applauded. This was the audience's first chance to get a look at the stars of the show—the charioteers. Some were greeted with loud cheers, reflecting the fact that drivers who won often became sports heroes with large

This Roman mosaic shows a charioteer and one of his horses. Victorious drivers often became national heroes who drew enormous crowds of adoring fans.

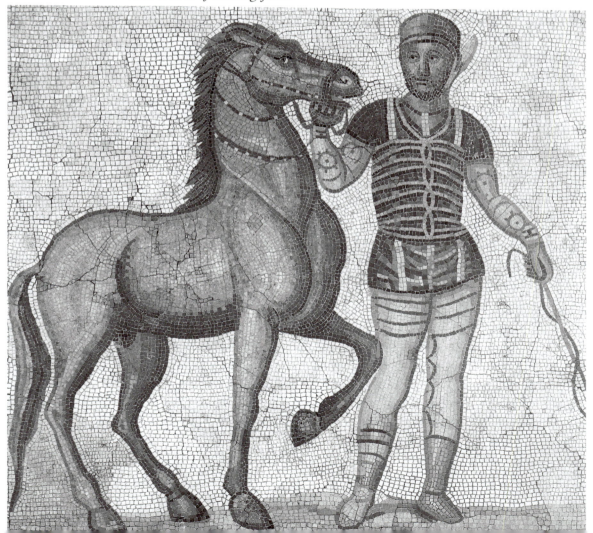

and devoted fan followings. These athletes, Jo-Ann Shelton writes,

> were admired by the men and adored by the women. Like movie stars today, they were recognized as they walked down the streets of Rome and greeted with swoons and squeals of delight. They were wined and dined by the wealthy and even by emperors.[73]

As revealed by ancient inscriptions, one of the most famous and beloved of these racing heroes, a man called Scorpus, won more than 2,000 races before dying in a track accident at age twenty-six. Another inscription tells about a driver named Calpurnianus, winner of 1,127 races. Even more impressive was the career of a popular charioteer named Gaius Appuleius Diocles, who bragged about his accomplishments on a monument he erected himself. "He drove first for the White faction, beginning in A.D. 122," he begins, speaking about himself in the third person,

> and won his first victory in A.D. 124 for the same faction. . . . He drove four-horse chariots for 24 years. He had 4,257 starts, with 1,462 first-place finishes, 110 of them in opening races. In single-entry races, he had 1,064 first-place finishes, winning 92 major purses, 32 of them worth 30,000 *sesterces* . . . 28 of them worth 40,000 *sesterces* . . . 29 worth 50,000 *sesterces* . . . and three worth 60,000 *sesterces*. . . . All total, he was in the money 2,900 times. . . . In races for two-horse chariots, he had 3 first-place finishes, 1 tie with the Whites, and 2 with the Greens. . . . In 815 races, he took the lead at the start and held it to the end. In 67 races, he came from behind to win. . . . He made nine horses hundred-race winners and one horse a two-hundred-race winner.[74]

This inscription mentions several important aspects and realities of Roman chariot racing. First, the author says that he won many of his victories on four-horse chariots (*quadrigae*), which is not surprising since this was the most common type of racing vehicle. Diocles also mentions taking part in a much smaller number of races for two-horse chariots (*bigae*). Less common were races for chariots with three horses or more than four horses. And for a diversion, from time to time the fans were treated to an offbeat race in which two men stood in each chariot; when one vehicle crossed the finish line, one of its occupants jumped out and ran at top speed once around the *euripus*.

Stables, Colors, and Fans

In his inscription, Diocles also mentions the "Whites" and the "Greens," calling them factions. The factions (*factiones*) were rival racing organizations, or private stables, owned by businessmen. An owner made some of his money by renting out his horses, equipment, and drivers to the government official who supervised the races and the rest by collecting the purses earned by any of his drivers who won races. The drivers received only a small portion of the purses because they were employees rather than free agents. A faction was therefore "a large organization," J.P.V.D. Balsdon, writes.

The Curse of the Demon

Often Roman charioteers hoped to gain an extra advantage over their opponents by invoking evil spirits and placing curses on other drivers. A number of such curses, in the form of inscriptions carved in stone, have been found. This one (quoted in Jo-Ann Shelton's As the Romans Did *) was discovered in a Roman town in northern Africa, an area in which chariot racing was particularly popular.*

I call upon you, o demon, whoever you are, and ask that from this hour, from this day, from this moment, you torture and kill the horses of the Green and the White factions, and that you kill and crush completely the drivers Clarus, Felix, Primulus, and Romanus, and that you leave not a breath in their bodies.

The staff . . . included numbers of highly skilled specialists, for the organization bought and owned its own race horses; it must constantly have commissioned new chariots and have seen that its chariots and their equipment were in first-class order; and it was in the market the whole time for the best drivers, who were either brought to Rome from the provinces or else were slaves or freedmen. . . . A vast staff was employed by each of the factions—buyers, trainers, doctors, horse-doctors, harness-men, [and] grooms. [75]

As for the colors, each faction was identified by the color of the tunics worn by its charioteers. In addition to the Whites and Greens, the four standard faction colors included the Reds and the Blues. By the early Roman Empire, the Greens and Blues were overall the most popular of the four. Like today's major-league football and other big sports teams, each stable enjoyed the general admiration and loyalty of a certain percentage of the populace.

In addition, there was a hard-core group of devotees, called partisans, for each faction. Their numbers were small—perhaps a few hundred to a thousand for each color. They usually sat in a block in the circus stands and made a loud commotion in support of their favorite drivers. Whether general supporters or die-hard partisans, fans could sometimes be fanatical, which raised the ire of a few intellectuals who felt that the racing scene was low class and childish. Pliny the Younger wrote that he could understand making a fuss over the speed of the horses or the drivers' skills. "But in fact," he asserts,

it is the racing-colors they [the fans] really support and care about, and if the colors were to be exchanged in mid-course during a race, they would transfer their favor and enthusiasm and rapidly desert the famous drivers and horses whose names they shout as they recognize them from afar. Such is the popularity of a worthless shirt—I don't mean with the crowd, which is worth less than the shirt, but with certain serious individuals. When I think of how this futile, tedious, monotonous business can keep them sitting endlessly in their seats, I take pleasure in the fact that their pleasure is not mine.[76]

Racing Strategies and Tactics

Most Romans completely disagreed with Pliny. Feeling that the races were far from

"futile" and "monotonous," they often became anxious to see the *pompa* end and the races begin. Before the start of the first race, however, the drivers had to hold a lottery to determine their starting positions. An official placed four different-colored balls in an urn, shook the container, and then poured the balls into four bowls. Each bowl represented one of four starting positions—one hugging the central *euripus,* two in the middle, and the last on the outside against the stands.

Finally, the charioteers took their positions and the first race began. As the chariots sprang outward onto the track, each driver tried to gain the advantage any way he could, although there were some common and effective general strategies

Another view of the Jerusalem Circus in the movie Ben-Hur *shows the competing chariots rounding one end of the massive* euripus, *which is adorned with statues.*

The Difficulties of Preparing the Racetrack

This account of the difficulties the makers of the 1959 version of Ben-Hur *encountered in preparing the track for and also shooting the film's famous chariot race is from John H. Humphrey's* Roman Circuses. *Except for the aspect of the cameras, the ancient Romans must have dealt with these same problems.*

In the absence of detailed information from archaeological or literary sources about the construction of the track-bed in the Circus Maximus, we may . . . draw upon the experience of the producers of *Ben-Hur.* . . . The composition of the track proved for them a considerable problem. It was originally constructed with a layer of ground rock debris which was steam-rollered into position; that was covered with a layer of ground lava, ten inches thick, which in turn was covered with a layer of crushed yellow rock eight inches thick. This was done because the track needed to be hard enough to hold the careening horses and chariots yet soft enough . . . not to lame the horses (as a more cemented upper surface would have done). The producers also discovered that the track required a drainage system in case of rain. However, once the track had been prepared in this manner, it was found that the horses were slowed too much. Thus, after only one day's trial, the crushed yellow rock and much of the layer of lava below were removed, leaving only one and a half inches of crushed lava as the new uppermost layer. . . . The resulting track-bed was far more serviceable, enabling the chariots to skid effectively around the corners. . . . Special contact lenses had to be made for the participants because of the dust and stones thrown up during the race. Indeed, to help cope with the problem facing the photographers, the track was smoothed and watered down after every take. However, the producers could not altogether dispose of the problem whereby the camera car slipped into the furrows or ruts made by the preceding chariot wheels.

and tactics. The drivers, Roland Auguet explains,

were less anxious to go fast than to be well placed, for the charioteer's art consisted mainly in hindering his rival without letting him do likewise. It was clearly an advantage to run "on the rails," along the *spina,* which was the shortest distance. If one of two competitors running abreast towards the rail managed to gain a few lengths, he would fall back and break the impetus of his rival, forcing him to slow down and lose time. . . . The charioteer who took too wide a sweep [on the turns] lost several seconds or even . . . found himself drifting towards the stands out of the line of the race, a clumsiness which at once called down the boos of the spectators. But to keep too close to the boundary-mark involved an even greater danger, that of smashing the chariot against it or having it overturned. . . . The chariots . . . were so fragile that the least shock could cause a catastrophe.[77]

The worst of such catastrophes was the "shipwreck" (*naufragium*), in which a chariot and its horses crashed into a mass of twisted debris and broken bones.

Only a single detailed ancient account of a Roman chariot race has survived, a tract by a fifth-century poet, Sidonius Apollinaris. The race he describes featured four chariots, one driven by his friend Consentius and a second by another charioteer from Consentius's faction. In these excerpts, which include a shipwreck, the action picks up several seconds after the chariots have left the starting gates.

The chariots fly out of sight [i.e., behind the *euripus*], quickly covering the long open stretch. . . . When they have come around the far turn, both the rival teams have passed Consentius, but his partner is in the lead. The middle teams concentrate now on taking the lead in the inside lane. . . . Consentius, however, redoubles his efforts to hold back his horses and skillfully reserve their energy for the seventh and last lap. The others race full out, urging their horses with whip and voice. . . . And thus they race, the first lap, the second, the third, the fourth.

. . . When the sixth lap [is] completed . . . Consentius . . . suddenly loosens the reins, plants his feet firmly on the floorboard, leans far over the chariot . . . and makes his fast horses gallop full out. One of the other drivers tries to make a very sharp turn at the far post, feeling Consentius close on his heels, but he is unable to turn his four wildly excited horses, and they plunge out of control. . . . The fourth driver . . . turns his galloping horses too far right toward the stands. Consentius drives straight and fast and passes [him]. . . . The latter pursues Consentius recklessly, hoping to overtake him. He cuts in sharply across the track. His horses lose their balance and fall. Their legs become tangled in the spinning chariot wheels and are snapped and broken. The driver is hurled headlong out of the shattered chariot which then falls on top of him in a heap of twisted wreckage. His broken and bloody body is still [i.e., he is dead]. And now the emperor presents the palm branch of victory to Consentius.[78]

Reenacting Classic Sea Battles

In the *ludi circenses,* the term shipwreck was used figuratively, whereas the largest of all Roman spectacles, the *naumachiae,* witnessed *real* shipwrecks. Most of these mock naval battles were staged on lakes, but sometimes the sponsor of the event ordered a special basin dug, obviously a huge and expensive undertaking. For example, Julius Caesar presented a *naumachia* in 46 B.C. in

This fanciful engraving depicts ships fighting in a flooded amphitheater. Most historians think such flooding was very uncommon, if it happened at all.

a large basin excavated in Rome's southwestern sector, near the Tiber River.

The possibility exists that these battles also took place on occasion in amphitheaters whose arenas had been temporarily flooded. Martial and other ancient writers mention the flooding of the Colosseum for this purpose in the late first century A.D. Some modern scholars reject this notion, saying that the mechanical difficulties involved in filling and draining the arena were too formidable. However, some recent evidence suggests that Roman engineers were able to flood the Colosseum at least once. If so, this was probably the incident to which Martial refers.

No matter where they were staged, all *naumachiae* featured vessels manned by criminals and war captives, who customarily fought to the death. Most often these men wore costumes representing the fighters in famous naval battles of past ages. Perhaps most popular and frequently staged was the fateful encounter between the Greeks and the Persians at Salamis in 480 B.C. (which saved Europe from Persian domination).

As for the numbers of ships and men involved in such a show, Augustus claimed he presented one (in 2 B.C.) in which thirty warships "and in addition a great number of smaller vessels" fought. "On board these fleets, exclusive of rowers," he adds, "there were about 3,000 combatants." [79] Much larger numbers of ships and men took part in the *naumachia* presented by one of Augustus's descendants, the emperor Claudius, in A.D. 52 (which may have been the largest mock naval battle ever staged). Tacitus left behind this account:

> A tunnel through the mountain between the Fucine Lake and the River Liris [several miles southeast of Rome] had now been completed. To enable a large crowd to see this impressive achievement, a naval battle was staged on the lake itself, like the exhibition given by Augustus on his artificial lake

105

An Epitaph for a Hero

In one of his epigrams (from D.R. Shackleton Bailey's translation), Martial wrote this epitaph for the famous charioteer Scorpus, who died young.

Let sad Victory break the palms of Idumaea [a region in Palestine known for its beautiful palm trees]. Favor, beat your bare breast with merciless hand. Let Honor put on mourning [clothes]. Grieving Glory, cast your crowned tresses on the unkind flames. Ah villainy! Scorpus, cheated of your first youth, you die. So soon you yoke black horses [symbolizing death]. The goal, ever quickly gained by your hastening car [chariot]—your life's goal too, why was it so close [i.e., why did your life hasten to its end as quickly as your chariot rushed for the finish line]?

adjoining the Tiber, though his ships and combatants had been fewer. Claudius equipped warships manned with nineteen thousand combatants, surrounding them with a circle of rafts [loaded with soldiers] to prevent their escape. Enough space in the middle, however, was left for energetic rowing, skillful steering, charging, and all the incidents of a sea-battle. . . . The coast, the slopes, and the hill-tops were thronged like a theater by innumerable spectators, who had come from the neighboring towns and even from Rome itself—to see the show. . . . Claudius presided in a splendid military cloak. . . . Though the fighters were criminals, they fought like brave men. After much blood-letting, they were spared extermination.[80]

As time went on, the vast expense of these spectacles made staging them increasingly difficult and eventually impractical. The last known *naumachia* took place in 248 at the games celebrating Rome's thousandth birthday. By contrast, the chariot races continued well past that date. They even survived the fall of the western Roman Empire and for centuries to come remained a staple form of entertainment in Constantinople, capital of the eastern Roman realm. Only in the twelfth century did the circus races end. The reason was the same as for the demise of the naval battles—no one could afford to stage them anymore.

Most of the leisure pursuits the Romans enjoyed have survived, however. People still play ball, throw dinner parties, attend plays and boxing matches, hunt, go to the beach, and gamble. They also read novels, poetry, and historical studies, now and then including books like this one about the long vanished Romans and how they enjoyed their free time.

Notes

Introduction: How Do We Know About Roman Leisure Pursuits?

1. J.P.V.D. Balsdon, *Life and Leisure in Ancient Rome.* New York: McGraw-Hill, 1969, p. 13.
2. Quoted in Jo-Ann Shelton, ed., *As the Romans Did: A Sourcebook in Roman Social History.* New York: Oxford University Press, 1988, p. 344.
3. Quoted in Robert B. Kebric, *Roman People.* Mountain View, CA: Mayfield, 2001, p. 202.

Chapter 1: The Roman Baths

4. Tacitus, *The Annals,* published as *The Annals of Ancient Rome,* trans. Michael Grant. New York: Penguin Books, 1989, pp. 322–23.
5. Quoted in Elaine Fantham et al., *Women in the Classical World.* New York: Oxford University Press, 1994, p. 334.
6. Pliny the Younger, *Letters,* published as *The Letters of the Younger Pliny,* trans. Betty Radice. New York: Penguin Books, 1969, p. 76.
7. Lucian, *The Bath,* in *Roman Civilization, Selected Readings,* vol. 2, *The Empire,* ed. Naphtali Lewis and Meyer Reinhold. New York: Columbia University Press, 1990, pp. 140–41.
8. Lucian, *The Bath,* p. 141.
9. Aelius Spartianus (likely a pseudonym), *Hadrian,* in *Augustan History,* published as *Lives of the Later Caesars, the First Part of the* Augustan History, *with Newly Compiled* Lives *of Nerva and Trajan,* trans. Anthony Birley. New York: Penguin Books, 1976, p. 76.
10. Martial, *Epigrams.* Ed. and trans. D.R. Shackleton Bailey. 3 Vols. Cambridge, MA: Harvard University Press, 1993, p. 225, Vol. 1.
11. Seneca, *Letters,* quoted in Shelton, *As the Romans Did,* p. 314.
12. Seneca, *Letters,* quoted in Shelton, *As the Romans Did,* p. 314.

Chapter 2: The Art of the Dinner Party

13. Martial, *Epigrams,* vol. 1, p. 153.
14. Martial, *Epigrams,* vol. 2, p. 39.
15. Ammianus Marcellinus, *History,* published as *The Later Roman Empire,* A.D. *354–378,* ed. and trans. Walter Hamilton. New York: Penguin Books, 1986, p. 360.
16. Pliny the Younger, *Letters,* pp. 48–49.

17. Juvenal, *Satires,* published as *The Sixteen Satires,* trans. Peter Green. New York: Penguin Books, 1974, p. 227.
18. Pliny the Younger, *Letters,* pp. 63–64.
19. Catullus, complete poems, in *The Poems of Catullus,* ed. and trans. Guy Lee. New York: Oxford University Press, 1990, p. 15.
20. Pliny the Younger, *Letters,* p. 154.
21. Martial, *Epigrams,* vol. 1, p. 237.
22. Pliny the Younger, *Letters,* p. 255.
23. Cicero, *On Duties,* trans. Margaret Atkins. New York: Cambridge University Press, 1991, p. 52.

Chapter 3: Diverse Theatrical Displays

24. Oscar G. Brockett, *History of the Theater.* Boston: Allyn and Bacon, 1982, p. 56.
25. Edith Hamilton, *The Roman Way to Western Civilization.* New York: W.W. Norton, 1932, pp. 9–10.
26. Hamilton, *The Roman Way,* p. 16.
27. Balsdon, *Life and Leisure in Ancient Rome,* p. 271.
28. Terence, *The Eunuch,* in *Terence: The Comedies,* trans. Betty Radice. New York: Penguin Books, 1976, p. 166.
29. Terence, *The Mother-in-Law,* in *Terence: The Comedies,* pp. 293–94.
30. Apuleius, *The Golden Ass,* trans. P.G. Walsh. Oxford, UK: Oxford University Press, 1994, p. 215.
31. Pliny the Younger, *Letters,* p. 46.

Chapter 4: Roman Tastes in Literature

32. Hamilton, *The Roman Way,* p. 9.
33. R.H. Barrow, *The Romans.* Baltimore: Penguin Books, 1949, p. 113.
34. Quoted in Shelton, *As the Romans Did,* p. 166.
35. Quoted in Bernard Knox, ed., *The Norton Book of Classical Literature.* New York: W.W. Norton, 1993, pp. 735–36.
36. Quoted in Knox, *Norton Book of Classical Literature,* pp. 718–19.
37. Quoted in Meyer Reinhold, *Essentials of Greek and Roman Classics.* Great Neck, NY: Barron's, 1946, pp. 317–18.
38. Martial, *Epigrams,* vol. 2, p. 47.
39. Martial, *Epigrams,* vol. 2, p. 179.
40. Martial, *Epigrams,* vol. 1, p. 161.
41. Martial, *Epigrams,* vol. 1, p. 191.
42. Barrow, *The Romans,* p. 115.
43. Livy, *The History of Rome from Its Foundation,* books 1–5 published as *Livy: The Early History of Rome,* trans. Aubrey de Sélincourt. New York: Penguin Books, 1971, p. 34.
44. Pliny the Younger, *Letters,* p. 35.

Chapter 5: Games and Sporting Activities

45. Petronius, *Satyricon,* trans. J.P. Sullivan. New York: Penguin Books, 1977, p. 45.
46. Pliny the Younger, *Letters,* p. 141.
47. Balsdon, *Life and Leisure in Ancient Rome,* p. 156.
48. Quoted in Shelton, *As the Romans Did,* p. 309.
49. Waldo E. Sweet, ed., *Sport and Recreation in Ancient Greece: A Sourcebook with Translations.* New York: Oxford University Press, 1987, p. 108.

50. Pliny the Younger, *Letters*, p. 39.
51. Quoted in Sweet, *Sport and Recreation in Ancient Greece*, p. 158.
52. Pliny the Younger, *Letters*, p. 141.
53. Pliny the Younger, *Letters*, p. 254.

Chapter 6: Blood in the Sand: The Gladiators

54. Alan Baker, *The Gladiator: The Secret History of Rome's Warrior Slaves*. New York: St. Martin's, 2000, p. 4.
55. Eckart Kohne, ed., *Gladiators and Caesars: The Power of Spectacle in Ancient Rome*. Berkeley and Los Angeles: University of California Press, 2000, p. 37.
56. Kohne, *Gladiators and Caesars*, pp. 48–51.
57. Baker, *The Gladiator*, pp. 39–40.
58. Michael Grant, *Gladiators*. New York: Delacorte, 1967, p. 77.
59. Petronius, *Satyricon*, pp. 59–60.
60. Baker, *The Gladiator*, p. 85.
61. Baker, *The Gladiator*, pp. 172–73.

Chapter 7: Arena Hunters and Their Prey

62. Roland Auguet, *Cruelty and Civilization: The Roman Games*. London: Routledge, 1994, p. 81.
63. Pliny the Elder, *Natural History*, excerpted in *Pliny the Elder: Natural History: A Selection*, trans. John H. Healy. New York: Penguin Books, 1991, pp. 109–10, 112.
64. Auguet, *Cruelty and Civilization*, p. 89.
65. Martial, *Epigrams*, vol. 1, p. 25.
66. Martial, *Epigrams*, vol. 1, p. 23.
67. Quoted in Shelton, *As the Romans Did*, p. 387.
68. Pliny the Elder, *Natural History*, pp. 111–12.
69. Auguet, *Cruelty and Civilization*, p. 92.
70. Pliny the Elder, *Natural History*, pp. 108–109.
71. Martial, *Epigrams*, vol. 1, p. 19.

Chapter 8: Chariot Races and Mock Naval Battles

72. Richard C. Beacham, *Spectacle Entertainments of Early Imperial Rome*. New Haven, CT: Yale University Press, 1999, p. 22.
73. Shelton, *As the Romans Did*, p. 359.
74. Quoted in Shelton, *As the Romans Did*, p. 356.
75. Balsdon, *Life and Leisure in Ancient Rome*, p. 315.
76. Pliny the Younger, *Letters*, p. 236.
77. Auguet, *Cruelty and Civilization*, pp. 129–30.
78. Quoted in Shelton, *As the Romans Did*, pp. 351–52.
79. Augustus, *Res gestae*, in *Roman Civilization, Selected Readings*, vol. 1, *The Republic and Augustan Age*, ed. Naphtali Lewis and Meyer Reinhold. New York: Columbia University Press, 1990, p. 569.
80. Tacitus, *Annals*, p. 277.

Glossary

acroama: The collective name for music and literary readings at a fashionable dinner party.

amphitheater (in Latin, *amphitheatrum,* meaning "double theater"): A wooden or stone structure, usually oval shape and open at the top, in which the ancient Romans staged public games and shows, including gladiatorial fights.

andabates: Gladiators who fought while blindfolded by helmets with no eye holes.

apodyterium: In a bathhouse, a room for undressing and dressing.

apophoreta: Leftovers from a meal.

aretalogus: A person who told amusing or thought-provoking stories at a dinner party or other gathering.

as **(plural, *asses*):** A copper coin worth one-fourth of a sestertius.

Atellan farces (*Fabula Atellana*): Roman theatrical farces based on Greek models.

balneator: "Bathman"; the manager of a bathhouse or a bath attendant.

bestiarius **(plural, *bestiarii*):** "Beast man"; an arena hunter who may have had a lower status or used a different fighting style than a *venator*.

bigae: Chariots drawn by two horses.

calcei: Outdoor shoes.

caldarium: In a bathhouse, a "hot" room containing one or more warm pools.

cena: Dinner; the main meal.

comoedus: A person who recited passages from classic literature at a dinner party or other gathering.

confectores: "Executioners"; armed men who finished off wounded animals in the arena hunts.

denarius (plural, *denarii*): A silver coin worth one-twenty-fifth of an *aureas*.

dimachaeri: Gladiators who fought without shields, using two swords, one in each hand.

equites: Gladiators who fought on horseback.

essedarii: Gladiators who fought from moving chariots.

euripus **(or *spina*):** The long stone axis, decorated with obelisks and statues, that ran down the center of a Roman circus.

fabula saltica: The art or performance of Roman pantomime, which was similar to modern ballet.

factiones: "Factions"; chariot racing organizations or stables.

follis: A large, light ball inflated with air.

frigidarium: In a bathhouse, a "cold" room containing one or more cold pools.

gladiatrix: A woman gladiator.

gladius: The sword wielded by Roman soldiers and several types of gladiator and the word from which *gladiator* was derived.

gustus: The appetizers, or first course, of a dinner.

harpastum: A small hard ball; also a rough-and-tumble ball game that was perhaps similar to rugby.

histriones: Early Roman actors.

hoplomachus: A kind of gladiator similar to a Samnite, except armed with a shield and a spear in addition to a sword.

hypocaust: A heating system in which hot air from a furnace circulated through brick conduits into an open space beneath a building.

laconicum: In a bathhouse, a sauna, or warm and dry room.

laquearii: Gladiators whose principal weapon was the lasso.

lectus: A couch.

ludi circenses: Chariot races.

micatio: A gambling game in which a player tried to guess how many fingers his or her opponent would raise.

mime: A short comedic theatrical skit, often obscene; or an actor who performed such skits.

Morituri te salutant!: "Those about to die salute you!"; the phrase recited by gladiators just prior to combat.

munera (**singular,** *munus*): "Offerings" or "duties"; public shows involving gladiators.

myrmillo (**or** *murmillo*): "Fish man"; a kind of gladiator, similar to a Samnite but less heavily armored.

natatio: A swimming pool.

naufragium: "Shipwreck"; a disaster on a racetrack resulting from two or more chariots colliding and breaking up.

naumachia (**plural,** *naumachiae*): A staged sea battle.

noxii ad gladium ludi damnati: "Condemned to be killed by the sword in the games"; a death sentence to be carried out in the arena.

palaestrae: Gyms or wrestling areas, often housed in public bathhouses.

pantomimus: An actor who performed in a pantomime.

pastoral: Having to do with the countryside.

patronage: The system in which one individual, the client, gave homage to and did favors for a wealthier and more powerful person, the patron, in exchange for financial and legal protection.

phylakes: Greek theatrical farces, on which the Romans based their Atellan farces.

pompa: The paradelike ceremony that opened gladiatorial fights, chariot races, and other spectacles.

prima mensa: The second and main course of a dinner.

pulpitum: The stage in a Roman theater.

quadrigarum (**plural,** *quadrigae*): A chariot drawn by four horses.

retiarius (plural, *retiarii*): "Net wielder"; a kind of gladiator who wore little armor and carried a net and a long trident.

Samnite: A member of a fierce central Italian hill tribe conquered by the Romans during the early Republic; or a kind of gladiator attired as a Samnite warrior—heavily armored and carrying a sword and heavy shield.

scaenae frons: In a Roman theater, the wall behind the stage on which scenery was painted or hung.

scurra: "Jesters"; entertainers who told jokes and insulted the guests at a party.

scutum: The rectangular shield carried by Roman soldiers and also by certain gladiators, including the *myrmillones* and Samnites.

secunda mensa: The dessert, or third course, of a dinner.

secutor: A kind of gladiator, either the same as or very similar to a Samnite.

sestertius (plural, *sestertii* or *sesterces*): A silver or bronze coin originally equal to 2.5 asses and later 4, and also .25 of a denarius.

sica: A curved short sword wielded by Thracian warriors and gladiators.

sine missione: "To the death"; a kind of gladiatorial combat in which the combatants had to continue fighting until one was killed.

stans missus: Condition of a gladiator who attained a draw.

talis (plural, *tali*): The four-sided playing pieces used in the game knucklebones or as dice.

taurarius (plural, *taurarii*): An arena hunter who specialized in subduing and killing bulls.

tepidarium: In a bathhouse, a warm room in which a person waited a while before bathing in order to reduce the discomfort of passing too suddenly from the colder air outside the bathhouse into the muggy air in the heated rooms within.

thermarum (plural, *thermae*): A public bathhouse.

thermopolii (singular, *thermopolium*): Fast-food shops or snack bars.

Thracian: A native of the region of Thrace in Greece; or a Roman gladiator (also called a Thrax) who fought with a small round shield and short curved sword, traditional weapons of the early Thracians.

triclinium: A dining room.

trigon: A ball game in which three people tried to throw and catch one or more balls without dropping them.

unctorium: In a bathhouse, a room in which people rubbed themselves with oil after bathing.

velarium: An awning, such as the kind stretched over the top of a theater or amphitheater.

venationes (singular, *venatio*): "Hunts"; various kinds of animal shows that took place in amphitheaters.

venator (plural, *venatores*): "Hunter"; an arena performer who fought and killed animals.

vestis cenatoria (or *synthesis*): "Dinner suit"; a formal outfit worn to dinner parties and similar gatherings; it consisted of a tunic covered by a formal cloak.

For Further Reading

Books

Robert B. Kebric, *Roman People*. Mountain View, CA: Mayfield, 2001. This excellent volume by one of the leading scholars of ancient Rome contains an excellent, very readable chapter about Roman chariot racing.

John Malam, *Secret Worlds: Gladiators*. London: Dorling Kindersley, 2002. A beautifully illustrated book that brings the exciting but bloody gladiatorial combats of ancient Rome to life.

Anthony Marks and Graham Tingay, *The Romans*. London: Usborne, 1990. An excellent summary of the main aspects of Roman history, life, and arts, supported by hundreds of beautiful and accurate drawings reconstructing Roman times. Aimed at basic readers but highly recommended for anyone interested in Roman civilization.

Don Nardo, *Greek and Roman Theater*. San Diego: Lucent Books, 1995. This volume covers the less violent Roman entertainments, including plays, mimes, street theater, and poetry recitations.

———, *Roman Amphitheaters*. New York: Franklin Watts, 2002. Tells about the origins of the stone arenas where gladiators and animal hunters fought and often died, how these structures were built, and the variety of games they showcased.

Judith Simpson, *Ancient Rome*. New York: Time-Life, 1997. One of the best entries in Time-Life's library of picture books about the ancient world, this one is beautifully illustrated with attractive and appropriate photographs and paintings. The general but well-written text is aimed at intermediate younger readers.

Chester G. Starr, *The Ancient Romans*. New York: Oxford University Press, 1971. A clearly written survey of Roman history, featuring several interesting sidebars on such subjects as the Etruscans, Roman law, and the Roman army. It also contains many primary source quotes by Roman and Greek writers. For intermediate and advanced younger readers.

Websites

The Circuses: Roman Chariot Racing, Barbara F. McManus, College of New Rochelle (www.vroma.org). This is a well-written general overview of Roman chariot racing.

A Day at the Baths, PBS Secrets of Lost Empires (www.pbs.org). A virtual tour of a large Roman bathhouse, including recent photos of excavated sections of these structures.

Ludus Gladiatorius, English Reenactor Group (www.ludus.org. uk). The main page has many links that take the reader on a fascinating journey into modern attempts to restage ancient Roman gladiatorial bouts with authentic costumes, weapons, and tactics. Highly recommended.

Roman Dress, Illustrated History of the Roman Empire (www.roman-empire.net). A very informative site about everyday Roman clothing, supplemented by photos and drawings.

Major Works Consulted

Ancient Sources

Ammianus Marcellinus, *History*, published as *The Later Roman Empire, A.D. 354–378*. Ed. and trans. Walter Hamilton. New York: Penguin Books, 1986.

Apuleius, *The Golden Ass*. Trans. P.G. Walsh. Oxford, UK: Oxford University Press, 1994.

Augustan History, published as *Lives of the Later Caesars, the First Part of the* Augustan History, *with Newly Compiled Lives of Nerva and Trajan*. Trans. Anthony Birley. New York: Penguin Books, 1976.

Julius Caesar, *Commentary on the Gallic War* and *Commentary on the Civil War*, published as *War Commentaries of Caesar*. Trans. Rex Warner. New York: New American Library, 1960.

Catullus, complete poems, in *The Poems of Catullus*. Ed. and trans. Guy Lee. New York: Oxford University Press, 1990.

Cicero, various works collected in: *The Basic Works of Cicero*. Ed. Moses Hadas. New York: Random House, 1951; *Cicero: Murder Trials*. Trans. Michael Grant. New York: Penguin Books, 1990; *Cicero: The Nature of the Gods*. Trans. Horace C.P. McGregor. New York: Penguin Books, 1972; *Cicero: On Government*. Trans. Michael Grant. New York: Penguin Books, 1993; *Cicero: Selected Works*. Trans. Michael Grant. New York: Penguin Books, 1971; *Letters to Atticus*. 3 vols. Trans. E.O. Winstedt. Cambridge, MA: Harvard University Press, 1961; *Letters to His Friends*. 3 vols. Trans. W. Glynn Williams. Cambridge, MA: Harvard University Press, 1965; *On Duties*. Trans. Margaret Atkins. New York: Cambridge University Press, 1991; *Selected Political Speeches of Cicero*. Trans. Michael Grant. Baltimore: Penguin Books, 1979; and *Verrine Orations*. 2 vols. Trans. L.H.G. Greenwood. Cambridge, MA: Harvard University Press, 1966.

Dio Cassius, *Roman History: The Reign of Augustus*. Trans. Ian Scott-Kilvert. New York: Penguin Books, 1987.

Dionysius of Halicarnassus, *Roman Antiquities*. 7 vols. Trans. Earnest Cary. Cambridge, MA: Harvard University Press, 1963.

Fronto, *Correspondence*. 2 vols. Trans. C.R. Haines. Cambridge, MA: Harvard University Press, 1965.

Galen, various works in *Galen: Selected Works*. Trans. P.N. Singer. New York: Oxford University Press, 1997.

Francis R.B. Godolphin, ed., *The Latin Poets*. New York: Random House, 1949.

Juvenal, *Satires,* published as *The Sixteen Satires.* Trans. Peter Green. New York: Penguin Books, 1974.

Bernard Knox, ed., *The Norton Book of Classical Literature.* New York: W.W. Norton, 1993.

Naphtali Lewis and Meyer Reinhold, eds., *Roman Civilization, Selected Readings.* Vol. 1. *The Republic and Augustan Age,* and *Roman Civilization, Selected Readings.* Vol. 2. *The Empire.* New York: Columbia University Press, 1990.

Livy, *The History of Rome from Its Foundation.* Books 1–5 published as *Livy: The Early History of Rome.* Trans. Aubrey de Sélincourt. New York: Penguin Books, 1971; books 21–30 published as *Livy: The War with Hannibal.* Trans. Aubrey de Sélincourt. New York: Penguin Books, 1972; books 31–45 published as *Livy: Rome and the Mediterranean.* Trans. Henry Bettenson. New York: Penguin Books, 1976.

Martial, *Epigrams.* 3 vols. Ed. and trans. D.R. Shackleton Bailey. Cambridge, MA: Harvard University Press, 1993.

Ovid, *Metamorphoses.* Trans. Rolfe Humphries. Bloomington: University of Indiana Press, 1967; and selected poems in *Ovid: The Love Poems.* Trans. A.D. Melville. New York: Oxford University Press, 1990.

Petronius, *The Satyricon.* Trans. J.P. Sullivan. New York: Penguin Books, 1977.

Plautus, plays excerpted in *Plautus: "The Rope" and Other Plays.* Trans. E.F. Watling. New York: Penguin Books, 1964.

Pliny the Elder, *Natural History.* 10 vols. Trans. H. Rackham. Cambridge, MA: Harvard University Press, 1967; also excerpted in *Pliny the Elder: Natural History: A Selection.* Trans. John H. Healy. New York: Penguin Books, 1991.

Pliny the Younger, *Letters.* 2 vols. Trans. William Melmouth. Cambridge, MA: Harvard University Press, 1961; also *The Letters of the Younger Pliny.* Trans. Betty Radice. New York: Penguin Books, 1969.

Plutarch, *Parallel Lives,* published complete as *Lives of the Noble Grecians and Romans.* Trans. John Dryden. New York: Random House, 1932; also excerpted in *Fall of the Roman Republic: Six Lives by Plutarch.* Trans. Rex Warner. New York: Penguin Books, 1972; and *Makers of Rome: Nine Lives by Plutarch.* Trans. Ian Scott-Kilvert. New York: Penguin Books, 1965.

Seneca, *Letters,* published as *Seneca: Letters from a Stoic.* Trans. Robin Campbell. New York: Penguin Books, 1969; also *Moral Epistles.* 3 vols. Trans. Richard M. Gummere. Cambridge, MA: Harvard University Press, 1961; *Moral Essays.* 3 vols. Trans. John W. Basore. Cambridge, MA: Harvard University Press, 1963; and assorted works collected in *The Stoic Philosophy of Seneca.* Trans. and ed. Moses Hadas. New York: W.W. Norton, 1958; and *Seneca: Dialogues and Letters.* Trans. and ed. C.D.N. Costa. New York: Penguin Books, 1997.

Jo-Ann Shelton, ed., *As the Romans Did: A Sourcebook in Roman Social*

History. New York: Oxford University Press, 1988.

William G. Sinnegin, ed., *Sources in Western Civilization: Rome.* New York: Free, 1965.

Statius, *Works.* 2 vols. Trans. J.H. Mozley. Cambridge, MA: Harvard University Press, 1961.

Suetonius, *The Twelve Caesars.* Trans. Robert Graves. Rev. Michael Grant. New York: Penguin Books, 1979.

Waldo E. Sweet, ed., *Sport and Recreation in Ancient Greece: A Sourcebook with Translations.* New York: Oxford University Press, 1987.

Tacitus, *The Annals,* published as *The Annals of Ancient Rome.* Trans. Michael Grant. New York: Penguin Books, 1989.

Terence, complete surviving works in *Terence: The Comedies.* Trans. Betty Radice. New York: Penguin Books, 1976.

Virgil, *The Aeneid.* Trans. Patric Dickinson. New York: New American Library, 1961; and *The Aeneid.* Trans. David West. New York: Penguin Books, 1990; also *Works.* 2 vols. Trans. H. Rushton Fairclough. Cambridge, MA: Harvard University Press, 1967.

Modern Sources

Roland Auguet, *Cruelty and Civilization: The Roman Games.* London: Routledge, 1994. A commendable overview of Roman games, including gladiatorial combats, staged sea battles, wild beast hunts, chariot races, circus factions, and the layout of circuses and amphitheaters.

Alan Baker, *The Gladiator: The Secret History of Rome's Warrior Slaves.* New York: St. Martin's, 2000. An excellent general discussion of Roman gladiators, including the political and social dimensions of their combats as well as the kinds of fighters and how they fought. Highly recommended.

J.P.V.D. Balsdon, *Life and Leisure in Ancient Rome.* New York: McGraw-Hill, 1969. This huge, detailed, and masterful volume by a highly respected historian is one of the best general studies of Roman life, customs, and traditions. In addition to sections on exercise, festivals, arena games, wild animal shows, chariot races, and Greek sports (as practiced by the Romans), it contains fulsome discussions of Roman theater, mimes and pantomimes, children's games, family life, schooling, slavery, dining habits, public baths, and more.

Richard C. Beacham, *Spectacle Entertainments of Early Imperial Rome.* New Haven, CT: Yale University Press, 1999. This fine study of the famous Roman games is highlighted by first-class scholarship and an excellent bibliography.

James H. Butler, *The Theater and Drama of Greece and Rome.* San Francisco: Chandler, 1972. A useful general overview of ancient theater, including the playwrights and their works, the theater buildings, and the manner in which plays were performed.

Lionel Casson, *Libraries in the Ancient World.* New Haven, CT: Yale University Press, 2001. Casson, one of the leading classical scholars of the twentieth century, explores the great libraries of the ancient Near East (including the one in Alexandria), Greece, and Rome.

———, *Masters of Ancient Comedy*. New York: Macmillan, 1960. Another fine study by Casson, this book presents some excellent translations of plays by Plautus and Terence, along with informative commentary. Highly recommended.

———, *Travel in the Ancient World*. Baltimore: Johns Hopkins University Press, 1994. A classic of its kind, Casson's study of ancient travelers and their conveyances includes fulsome sections on Roman roads and the facilities that grew up along them. This is fascinating, rewarding reading that brings the ancient world to life.

Gian B. Conte, *Latin Literature: A History*. Trans. Joseph B. Solodow. Rev. Don P. Fowler and Glenn W. Most. Baltimore: Johns Hopkins University Press, 1999. A fine, up-to-date summary of the development of ancient Roman literature.

F.R. Cowell, *Life in Ancient Rome*. New York: G.P. Putnam's Sons, 1961. Cowell, one of the more noted modern experts on ancient Rome, here offers a commendable, easy-to-read study of most aspects of Roman daily life. Highly recommended.

Ilaria G. Giacosa, *A Taste of Ancient Rome*. Trans. Anna Herklotz. Chicago: University of Chicago Press, 1994. An excellent, tantalizing collection of Roman recipes inspired by those mentioned in ancient documents. It is highly recommended that the reader try some of these to get a real feel for what the Romans ate.

Jean-Claude Golvin, *Amphitheaters and Gladiators*. Paris: CNRS, 1990. The definitive modern work on ancient Roman amphitheaters, the structures built to house gladiatorial combats. Highly recommended for serious students of the subject.

Michael Grant, *Gladiators*. New York: Delacorte, 1967. One of the most prolific of modern classical historians delivers a highly comprehensive and readable general study of the subject.

———, *The World of Rome*. New York: New American Library, 1960. A scholarly yet colorful and fascinating glimpse of Roman culture, with plenty of primary source quotes revealing much about Roman life. Considered by many to be a modern classic of its kind.

John H. Humphrey, *Roman Circuses: Arenas for Chariot Racing*. Berkeley and Los Angeles: University of California Press, 1986. This large, scholarly volume, the most comprehensive and up-to-date study of Roman racing available, will appeal mainly to specialists in and serious buffs of Roman history and culture.

G.O. Hutchinson, *Latin Literature from Seneca to Juvenal: A Critical Study*. New York: Oxford University Press, 1993. A scholarly, information-packed look at the literature of the early Roman Empire.

Eckart Kohne, ed., *Gladiators and Caesars: The Power of Spectacle in Ancient Rome*. Berkeley and Los Angeles: University of California Press, 2000. An in-depth, insightful, very well written treatment of the subject. Highly recommended.

Joan Liversidge, *Everyday Life in the Roman Empire*. New York: G.P. Putnam's Sons, 1976. A well-researched and clearly written synopsis of most major aspects of Roman life, including leisure pursuits, consistently supported by references to various archaeological discoveries.

Thomas N. Mitchell, *Cicero: The Senior Statesman*. New Haven, CT: Yale University Press, 1991. An informative, up-to-date study of the great politician, orator, writer, courageous champion of the disintegrating Republic, and one of the most important and influential literary figures in Western history.

Vera Olivova, *Sport and Games in the Ancient World*. New York: St. Martin's, 1984. This large, well written volume begins with useful overviews of how experts think that sport originally evolved and athletic practices in the Near East and Egypt. The author then examines Greek sports, beginning with the Bronze Age and Homeric depictions, and concludes with Etruscan games and Roman festivals and games.

Michael B. Poliakoff, *Combat Sports in the Ancient World*. New Haven, CT: Yale University Press, 1987. Detailed, well written, and well documented, this is the definitive recent study of ancient wrestling, boxing, *pankration*, and other combat sports.

Additional Works Consulted

Lesley Adkins and Roy A. Adkins, *Handbook to Life in Ancient Rome*. New York: Facts On File, 1994.

R.H. Barrow, *The Romans*. Baltimore: Penguin Books, 1949.

Carlin A. Barton, *The Sorrow of the Ancient Romans: The Gladiator and the Monster*. Princeton, NJ: Princeton University Press, 1993.

William Beare, *The Roman Stage*. London: Methuen, 1968.

Herbert W. Benario, *An Introduction to Tacitus*. Athens: University of Georgia Press, 1975.

S.F. Bonner, *Education in Ancient Rome from the Elder Cato to the Younger Pliny*. London: Methuen, 1977.

A.J. Boyle, ed., *Roman Epic*. New York: Routledge, 1993.

Oscar G. Brockett, *History of the Theater*. Boston: Allyn and Bacon, 1982.

Matthew Bunson, *A Dictionary of the Roman Empire*. Oxford, UK: Oxford University Press, 1991.

Alan Cameron, *Circus Factions: Blues and Greens at Rome and Byzantium*. London: Clarendon, 1976.

Jerome Carcopino, *Daily Life in Ancient Rome: The People and the City at the Height of the Empire*. Rev. ed. New Haven, CT: Yale University Press, 1992.

Raymond Chevallier, *Roman Roads*. Trans. N.H. Field. Berkeley and Los Angeles: University of California Press, 1976.

J. White Duff, *A Literary History of Rome, from the Origins to the Close of the Golden Age*. New York: Barnes and Noble, 1960.

Will Durant, *Caesar and Christ: A History of Roman Civilization and of Christianity from Their Beginnings to A.D. 325*. New York: Simon and Schuster, 1944.

Elaine Fantham, *Roman Literary Culture: From Cicero to Apuleius*. Baltimore: Johns Hopkins University Press, 1996.

Elaine Fantham et al., *Women in the Classical World*. New York: Oxford University Press, 1994.

Alison Futrell, *Blood in the Arena: The Spectacle of Roman Power*. Austin: University of Texas Press, 1998.

Peter Garnsey, *Social Status and Legal Privilege in the Roman Empire*. Oxford, UK: Clarendon, 1970.

Marion Geisinger, *Plays, Players, and Playwrights: An Illustrated History of the Theater*. New York: Hart, 1971.

Michael Grant, *Greek and Latin Authors, 800 B.C.–A.D. 1000*. New York: H.W. Wilson, 1980.

———, *A Social History of Greece and Rome*. New York: Charles Scribner's Sons, 1992.

Edith Hamilton, *The Roman Way to Western Civilization*. New York: W.W. Norton, 1932.

Ian Jenkins, *Greek and Roman Life*. Cambridge, MA: Harvard University Press, 1986.

Harold W. Johnston, *The Private Life of the Romans*. New York: Cooper Square, 1973.

Otto Kiefer, *Sexual Life in Ancient Rome*. New York: Dorset, 1993.

R.O.A.M. Lyne, *The Latin Love Poets from Catullus to Horace*. Oxford, UK: Oxford University Press, 1980.

Alexander G. McKay, *Houses, Villas, and Palaces in the Roman World*. Baltimore: Johns Hopkins University Press, 1998.

Peter Quennell, *The Colosseum*. New York: Newsweek Book Division, 1971.

Meyer Reinhold, *Essentials of Greek and Roman Classics*. Great Neck, NY: Barron's, 1946.

Henry T. Rowell, *Rome in the Augustan Age*. Norman: University of Oklahoma Press, 1962.

Jon Solomon, *The Ancient World in the Cinema*. New Haven, CT: Yale University Press, 2001.

Chester G. Starr, *Civilization and the Caesars: The Intellectual Revolution in the Roman Empire*. New York: Norton, 1965.

Donald Strong, *Roman Crafts*. London: Duckworth, 1976.

Charles Van Doren, *A History of Knowledge, Past, Present, and Future*. New York: Ballantine Books, 1991.

P.G. Walsh, *Livy: His Historical Aims and Methods*. New York: Cambridge University Press, 1967.

Thomas E.J. Wiedemann, *Emperors and Gladiators*. London: Routledge, 1992.

L.P. Wilkinson, *The Roman Experience*. Lanham, MD: University Press of America, 1974.

Stephen Wisdom, *Gladiators: 100 B.C.–A.D. 200*. Oxford, UK: Osprey, 2001. (Nonscholars should be aware that the text of this volume, although useful in many ways, contains a considerable number of factual errors; they should, therefore, approach it with caution.)

Fikret Yegül, *Baths and Bathing in Classical Antiquity*. Cambridge, MA: MIT Press, 1992.

Index

Picture Credits

About the Author

Classical historian Don Nardo has published many volumes about ancient Roman history and culture, including *The Age of Augustus, A Travel Guide to Ancient Rome, Life of a Roman Gladiator,* and Greenhaven Press's massive *Encyclopedia of Greek and Roman Mythology.* Mr. Nardo also writes screenplays and teleplays and composes music. He lives in Massachusetts with his wife, Christine.